D0377012

pocket posh® JUMBLE® CrossWords™ 5

PLEASANT
WORDS
ARE AS A
HONEYCOMB
SWEET TO THE SOUL
AND
HEALTH
TO the
BONES
PROVERBS 16:24

pocket posh®

JUMBLE® CrossWords™ 5

David L. Hoyt

Andrews McMeel Publishing, LLC
Kansas City • Sydney • London

Pocket Posh® Jumble® Crosswords™ 5

Andrews McMeel Publishing, LLC
an Andrews McMeel Universal company
1130 Walnut Street, Kansas City, Missouri 64106

www.andrewsmcmeel.com
www.puzzlesociety.com

14 15 16 17 18 SHZ 10 9 8 7 6 5 4 3 2 1

ISBN: 978-1-4494-5037-3

HOW TO PLaY

Complete the crossword puzzle by looking at the clues and unscrambling the answers. When the puzzle is complete, unscramble the circled letters to solve the BONUS.

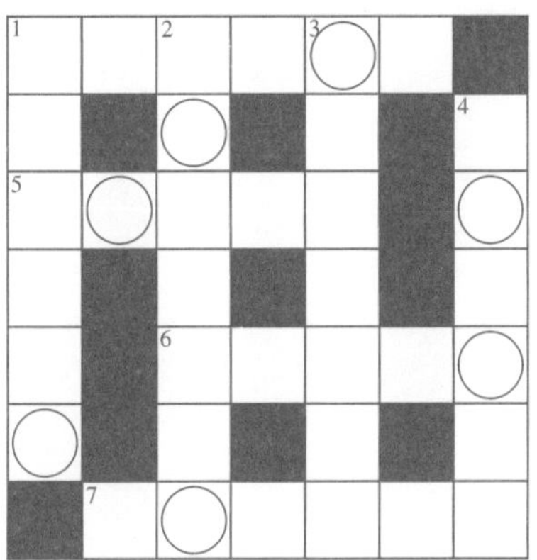

ACROSS

CLUE	ANSWER
1. Plan	EMCSEH
5. Game sayer	NMSIO
6. Sharp spine	HTONR
7. One of eight	RNUASU

DOWN

CLUE	ANSWER
1. ______ seed	MEESAS
2. Wheel spinner	AERHTSM
3. Type of storm	NOMSONO
4. Happenings	TNVSEE

CLUE: The Roman goddess of wisdom

BONUS ◯◯◯◯◯◯◯

JUMBLE® CrossWords™

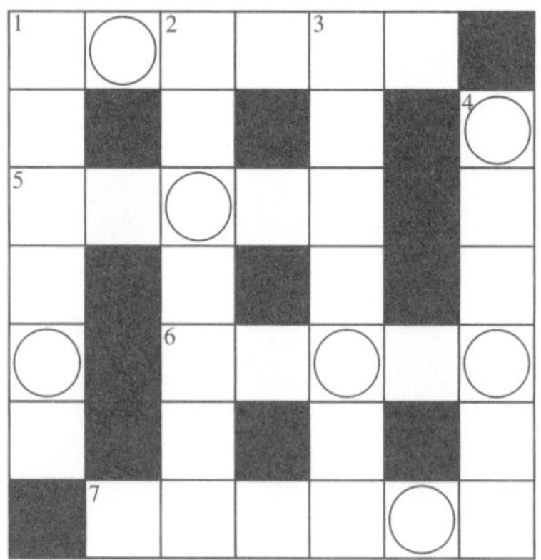

ACROSS

CLUE	ANSWER
1. Spread out	DENXAP
5. ______ practice	HRIOC
6. Accord	NIUNO
7. Performance structures	TSSGAE

DOWN

CLUE	ANSWER
1. Avoid	PACESE
2. Handiwork	ROPUDTC
3. ______ home	UNISGNR
4. Torments	TUNSHA

CLUE: A U.S. city and mythical creature

BONUS 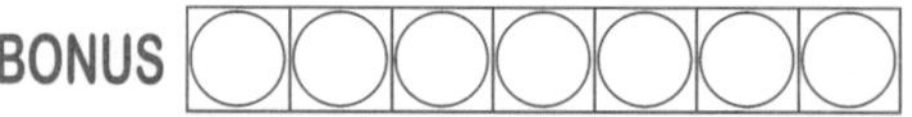

ACROSS

CLUE	ANSWER
1. The first of its kind	NSYADU
5. ______ pole	TMTEO
6. A musical instrument	ANOBJ
7. ______ in	ENPLIC

DOWN

CLUE	ANSWER
1. Irish ______	RTETSE
2. Distinguished	TONBAEL
3. Type of book	LCMANAA
4. Night ______	HOSCLO

BONUS **CLUE:** This woman's father co-founded the Simon & Schuster publishing company.

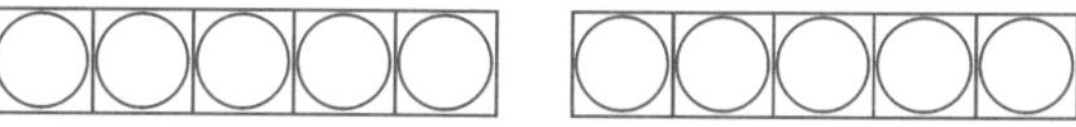

JUMBLE® CrossWords™

ACROSS

CLUE	ANSWER
1. Type of carnivore	AEWLES
5. A period of time	NTOMH
6. Youngster	UOTYH
7. Proofreader	DETIRO

DOWN

CLUE	ANSWER
1. Type of marsupial	MOWTAB
2. Bothered	NAONDEY
3. ______ pipe	HSXEUAT
4. Gates, to the rest	RCREIH

BONUS **CLUE:** This city, which is home to about 80,000 people, is home to a pro sport's hall of fame.

,
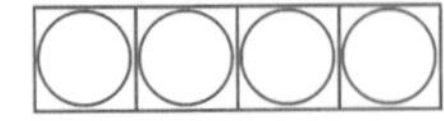

ACROSS

CLUE	ANSWER
1. A U.S.state capital	NSAIUT
5. Understand	RSGPA
6. Disturb	SPUTE
7. Membrane breaks	RELSUC

DOWN

CLUE	ANSWER
1. Irks	SGANER
2. Shoreline flyer	AGUESLL
3. Predicament	MSPSEAI
4. Type of plant	ACSUTC

BONUS

CLUE: Approximately 98 percent of this is covered with ice.

JUMBLE® CrossWords™

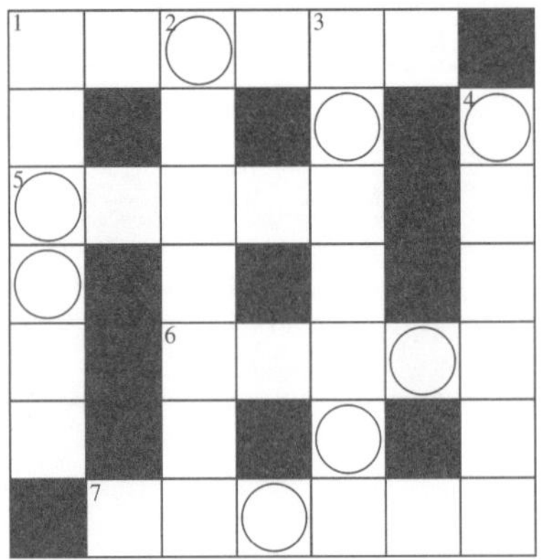

ACROSS

CLUE	ANSWER
1. Destructive animal	NVIERM
5. Destroyed	PKUTA
6. ______ circle	RNNIE
7. Respectable	TDENEC

DOWN

CLUE	ANSWER
1. Seafaring Scandinavian	KIVIGN
2. Type of animal	PEERITL
3. Deeply felt	NITNEES
4. Soul	PISITR

CLUE: ______ debuted on store shelves in 1930.

BONUS ◯◯◯◯◯◯◯◯

ACROSS

CLUE	ANSWER
1. ______ business	YKNOME
5. In the ______	RCALE
6. News ______	HFSAL
7. Eccentric people	LESFKA

DOWN

CLUE	ANSWER
1. Rourke or Rooney	MYCEIK
2. Required	ENDELUF
3. Designate	KAREAMR
4. Figure ______	ETSIHG

CLUE: This U.S. state is home to more lighthouses than any other.

BONUS 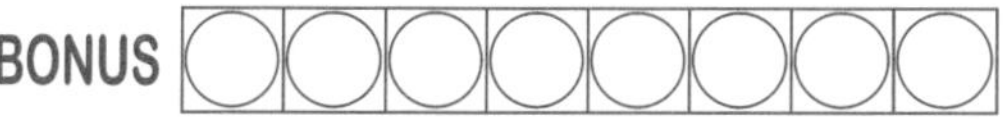

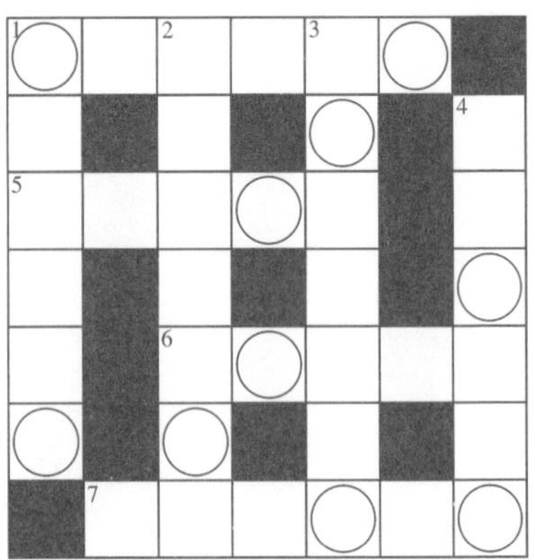

ACROSS

CLUE	ANSWER
1. Intelligently	LIESYW
5. Late	RATYD
6. Used to express wonder	LGYLO
7. Remained	ASTDEY

DOWN

CLUE	ANSWER
1. Quick-______	DTIWTE
2. Specter, ghost	PHRSGIT
3. Fidelity	YOLLAYT
4. Kept afloat	UEDBYO

BONUS

CLUE: This show was, at one time, one of the most popular children's shows on television.

ACROSS

CLUE	ANSWER
1. Small	TEPEIT
5. White ______	DBARE
6. Rose plant part	HNROT
7. A European city	ANEGEV

DOWN

CLUE	ANSWER
1. People	UICPLB
2. Type of beam	ELRETST
3. Pollywog	DATOPEL
4. Eye part	RCEAON

BONUS

CLUE: This actor, whose first name is the same as the last name of a U.S. president, was born in Ireland.

JUMBLE® CrossWords™

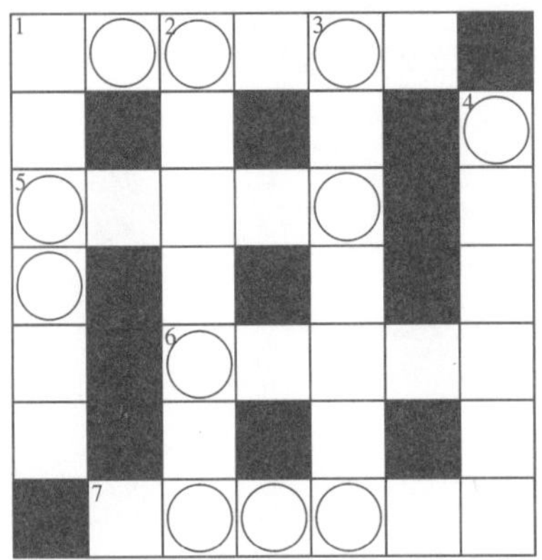

ACROSS

CLUE	ANSWER
1. Oriental philosopher	AUDDBH
5. Smoke or fog	PROAV
6. Seeped	ZOODE
7. Softer part of a seed	EKELRN

DOWN

CLUE	ANSWER
1. Animal classification	NBVEIO
2. Express grief for	PEDOLER
3. ______ line	RHOONZI
4. Type of shoe	ANLASD

BONUS

CLUE: The ______ ______ is approximately 300 miles long.

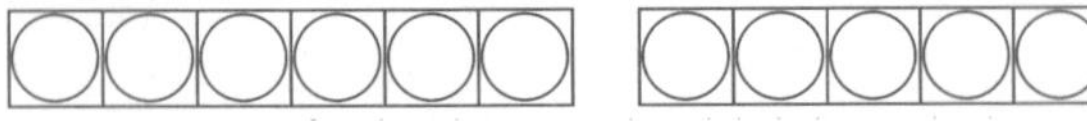

ACROSS

CLUE	ANSWER
1. Floor covering	PTCEAR
5. Type of flower	TLPIU
6. ______ Flynn	LEORR
7. Joiner	WREDEL

DOWN

CLUE	ANSWER
1. Strong-scented mint	TACPIN
2. Allay	LVEREIE
3. Elapsed	PERIXDE
4. Blacksmith's hammer	LUFREL

CLUE: This was developed in the 1940s but really took off in the 1950s.

BONUS

ACROSS

CLUE	ANSWER
1. Past	DBNEOY
5. Landing ______	PSIRT
6. Entertain	MESUA
7. Remove	TLDEEE

DOWN

CLUE	ANSWER
1. Type of rock	ATBSAL
2. Distance	RGYAADE
3. A Roman god	PEENUTN
4. Hinder	MEEIDP

CLUE: Charles Alfred founded his very successful company in 1872.

BONUS ○○○○○○○○○

ACROSS

CLUE	ANSWER
1. Weak	BEEELF
5. Rise	LMCIB
6. ______song	RCOTH
7. ______ Norton	WDDRAE

DOWN

CLUE	ANSWER
1. Looking at	FGNAIC
2. Thrown out	EEDCVIT
3. Neighbor to Guinea	BILRIAE
4. Moved slowly	NICDEH

BONUS

CLUE: 80 percent of all volcanic activity occurs ____ ____ ____.

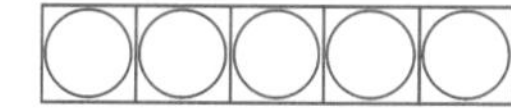

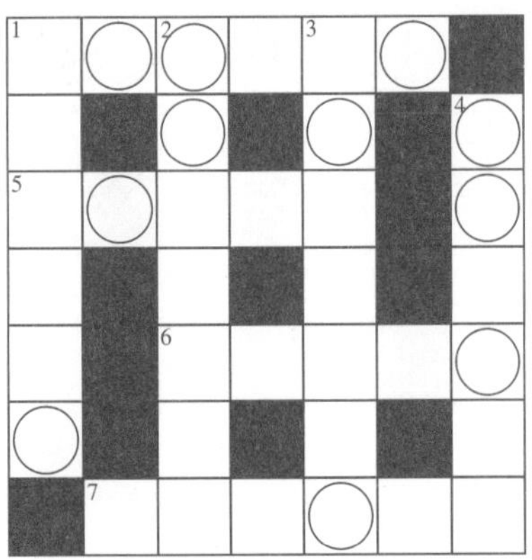

ACROSS

CLUE	ANSWER
1. Ranked	RAGEDD
5. Presents	TFGIS
6. ______ circle	NIREN
7. Pressure	RTSSSE

DOWN

CLUE	ANSWER
1. Laugh	LGGGIE
2. Beset	FALFCIT
3. Chief constituent	NEESCSE
4. An astrological sign	UTASRU

BONUS

CLUE: This performer, who died in 1987 at age 88, was voted the 19th "Greatest Movie Star of All Time" by *Entertainment Weekly*.

ACROSS

CLUE	ANSWER
1. Thief	TBIADN
5. Short in time	FRIBE
6. Swinging device	EGINH
7. Waxy stick	NROYAC

DOWN

CLUE	ANSWER
1. Chatter	EALBBB
2. Not either one	THINERE
3. Early childhood	FAYCINN
4. Block out	ERCNES

CLUE: Reasons for approximately 800,000 U.S. citizens each day to celebrate

BONUS

ACROSS

CLUE	ANSWER
1. Fixed	RDGIEG
5. Ground ______	LROFO
6. Bill ______	TGSEA
7. Annul	LNACEC

DOWN

CLUE	ANSWER
1. ______ ticket	FARELF
2. Country on the Black Sea	EIAGORG
3. Hit-or-miss	TARCEIR
4. Ship	LEESSV

CLUE: George de Mestral invented and patented this in 1955.

BONUS

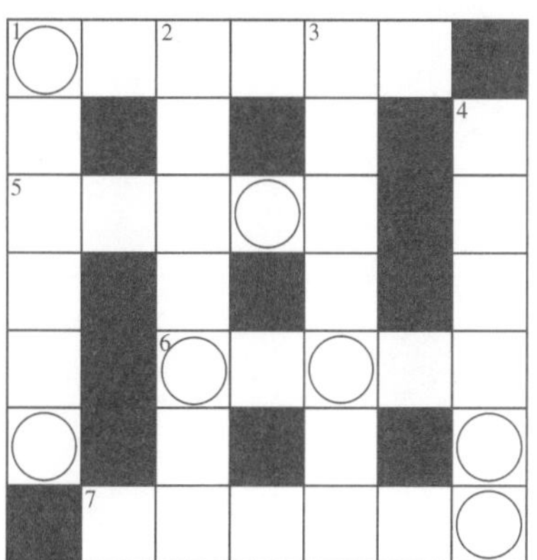

ACROSS

CLUE	ANSWER
1. Appearance to the eye	PSATCE
5. ______ cards	ROATT
6. ______ tree	LEIVO
7. Manner	TMDOEH

DOWN

CLUE	ANSWER
1. Sneak ______	KTCAAT
2. Function	RUPOPES
3. Scaleless fish	TSCIFHA
4. Protect	HISDLE

CLUE: Edwin Perkins invented this in 1927.

BONUS ◯◯◯◯ – ◯◯◯

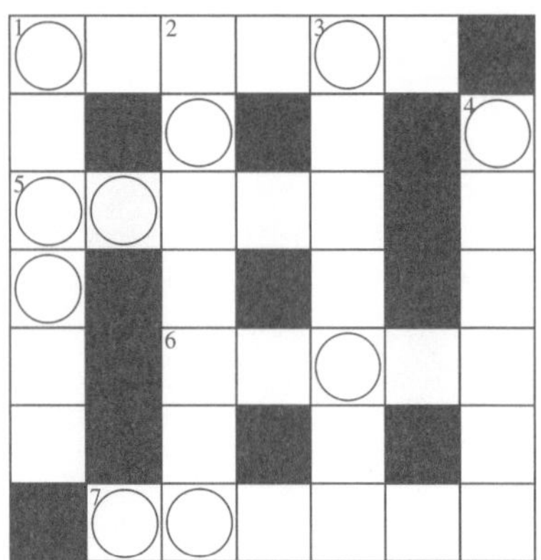

ACROSS

CLUE	ANSWER
1. Small unit of measure	MNIORC
5. Enter	PNITU
6. Optimal	EDILA
7. Closed	AESDEL

DOWN

CLUE	ANSWER
1. Sent	MIDAEL
2. ______ audience	PVACITE
3. ______ cookie	LATAOEM
4. Hit or caught	DEILAN

CLUE: This Irish-born actor worked as a truck driver, an assistant architect, and as a forklift operator for Guinness Brewery.

BONUS

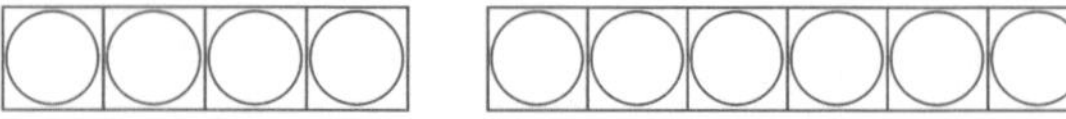

ACROSS

CLUE	ANSWER
1. Broadcast	TNYIFO
5. Snake _____	MNEVO
6. Bodies of water	LGSFU
7. Boring	DTSYGO

DOWN

CLUE	ANSWER
1. Beginner	EONCIV
2. Jay's time	TTHGOIN
3. Dropped	MFBUDEL
4. Active	RKYFIS

BONUS **CLUE:** The official state bird of Texas, Arkansas, Florida, Mississippi, and Tennessee

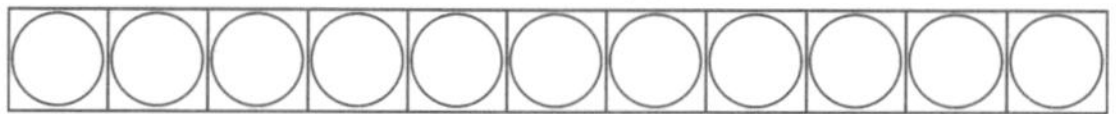

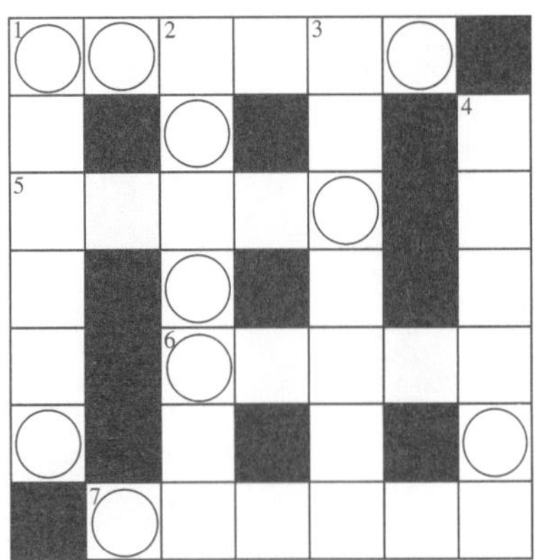

ACROSS

CLUE	ANSWER
1. Robert ______	DANOCR
5. Alarm	NRSIE
6. Chasm	BASYS
7. Stomach	EHLADN

DOWN

CLUE	ANSWER
1. ______ radiation	MSIOCC
2. Ideal condition	ANINAVR
3. Irritated	DAENYON
4. Long-running TV show	ASELIS

BONUS **CLUE:** This popular car was introduced in 1972.

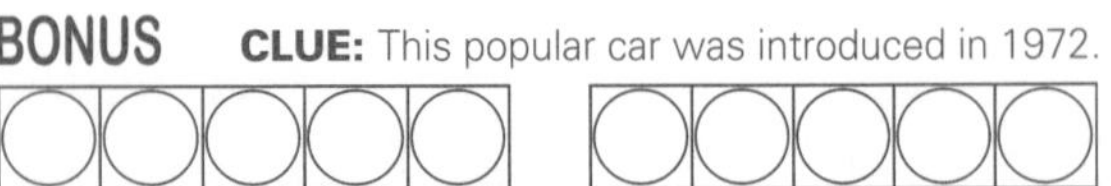

ACROSS

CLUE	ANSWER
1. Fictional tank engine	HOTSAM
5. ______ Wainwright	FRUSU
6. Sept., for example	NNHIT
7. Bank ______	LTRELE

DOWN

CLUE	ANSWER
1. Box ______	REUTTL
2. Violation	FSOEENF
3. Armory	RASNELA
4. Important player	HCARON

CLUE: The area now known as ______ was first settled by Paleo-Indians over 11,000 years ago.

BONUS ◯◯◯◯◯◯◯◯◯

ACROSS

CLUE	ANSWER
1. Harry ______	NMAOGR
5. Green ______	BHMTU
6. ______ beauty	NIENR
7. Legislature	TEESAN

DOWN

CLUE	ANSWER
1. Manner	DTEMOH
2. Usual	NOERIUT
3. European country	BILAAAN
4. Type of vehicle	AEHSRE

CLUE: Some varieties of this animal can live as long as 150 years.

BONUS ○○○○○○○○

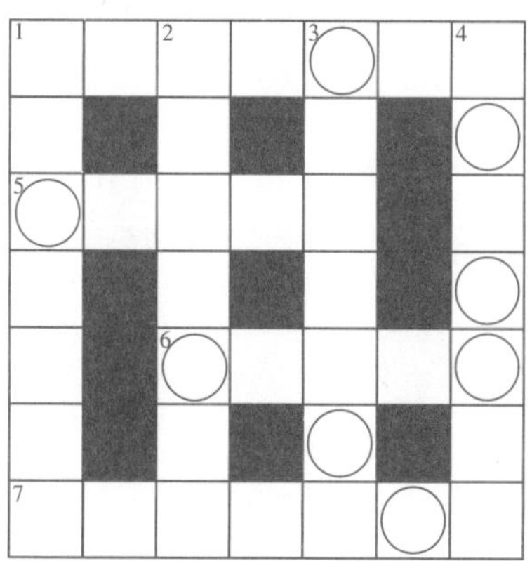

ACROSS

CLUE	ANSWER
1. Middle	UUELNSC
5. Grab	EESZI
6. Australian animal	LOKAA
7. Aboveboard	ECSRNIE

DOWN

CLUE	ANSWER
1. Lies close	NSLEETS
2. Yellow	KINEHCC
3. Raise	AEEETVL
4. ______ locker	TSORGEA

CLUE: In 2000, this show was listed in *The Guinness Book of Records* as having the most number of spin-off productions (including movies).

BONUS  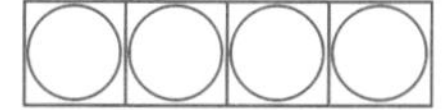

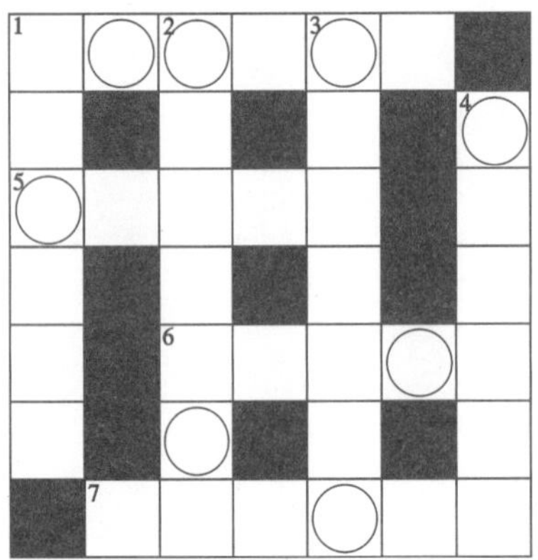

ACROSS

CLUE	ANSWER
1. Type of pastry	RELCIA
5. Confound	UTPSM
6. Pushed	REDOV
7. House ______	RTASER

DOWN

CLUE	ANSWER
1. Smoothly	LIYSAE
2. Clean	ALRENUD
3. Beg	PEOIMRL
4. Bona fide	ENTHOS

CLUE: The first electric ______ were developed in the early 1900s.

BONUS

ACROSS

CLUE	ANSWER
1. Storm _____	AGAMED
5. A place to eat	EIDNR
6. Rough game	YUBRG
7. Selected	EOSHNC

DOWN

CLUE	ANSWER
1. Sidestepped	DEODDG
2. Type of leader	MRACHNO
3. Shelters	AGGRASE
4. Mythical man	BAYNUN

CLUE: This island was first visited in the early 1500s.

BONUS ○○○○○○○

JUMBLE® CrossWords™

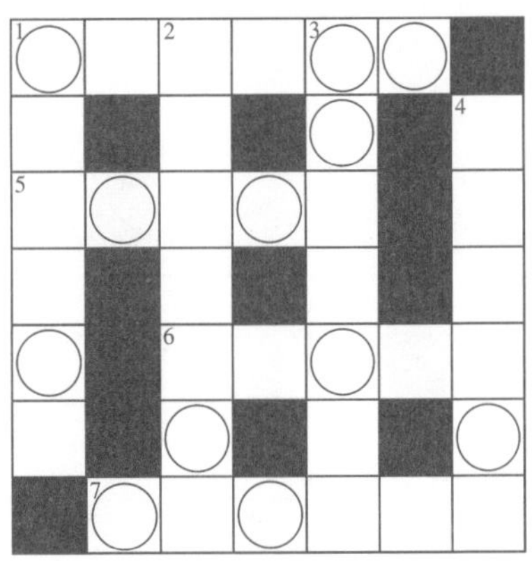

ACROSS

CLUE	ANSWER
1. Beefy	HKCNUY
5. ______ hat	REDYB
6. Chooser	TVREO
7. Copies	LESCNO

DOWN

CLUE	ANSWER
1. Trees	RECSAD
2. Fall apart	LNU·RVAE
3. Fictional planet	RYKPNOT
4. Incites	TASSTR

BONUS

CLUE: This fictional female was created in 1921.

ACROSS

CLUE	ANSWER
1. A bear, for example	MMLAAM
5. ______, MA	LASME
6. ______ circle	NIREN
7. Signal	NACOBE

DOWN

CLUE	ANSWER
1. Type of gun	KTMEUS
2. Depression	ALMISEA
3. Type of book	LAANAMC
4. Customer	TRPNOA

CLUE: This U.S. state capital was named for a German chancellor.

BONUS ○○○○○○○○

ACROSS

CLUE	ANSWER
1. The ______ system	RICTME
5. Goes across	APSNS
6. Edible plants	KELSE
7. Pens	TEWRIS

DOWN

CLUE	ANSWER
1. Overlooked	MEISDS
2. Type of vehicle	ERLIART
3. Scrutinize	PSNITCE
4. Stops	ASSCEE

CLUE: The smallest Nordic country

BONUS ○○○○○○○

ACROSS

CLUE	ANSWER
1. Strange	RCSWYE
5. Alfred ______	BONLE
6. Hurries	ASECR
7. Partner to blues	MRHHYT

DOWN

CLUE	ANSWER
1. Sensibly	NSALEY
2. New beginning	BIHRTRE
3. ______ strike	LIWCDTA
4. Aromatic resin	ASABML

BONUS

CLUE: Construction on the ______ ______ began in 1961.

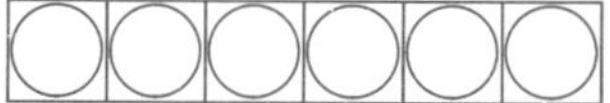

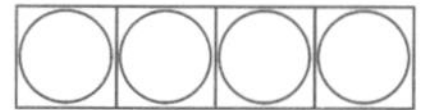

JUMBLE® CrossWords™

ACROSS

CLUE	ANSWER
1. Show	DITPCE
5. A man-made fiber	ARYNO
6. Blooper	RORER
7. Heisted	LONTSE

DOWN

CLUE	ANSWER
1. Steer	TIDCRE
2. House ______	PEYMANT
3. Remote ______	RTOLNOC
4. Small unit	RCMNIO

BONUS **CLUE:** The origin of this word dates back to ancient Greece.

ACROSS

CLUE	ANSWER
1. Miscellaneous item	NSYRDU
5. A sport	URYGB
6. '70s sitcom	DROAH
7. Forgive	NRADPO

DOWN

CLUE	ANSWER
1. Hot ______	TERSKA
2. A country	ANIREIG
3. Lovable TV character	DMYOARN
4. Get	BIOATN

BONUS **CLUE:** Fine

JUMBLE® CrossWords™

ACROSS

CLUE	ANSWER
1. Fastened, secured	DCLEOK
5. Bush	HRSBU
6. ______ Star	TONHR
7. 1. ______	RACSOS

DOWN

CLUE	ANSWER
1. Cataloged	LDIETS
2. Incessant	HIRCCNO
3. Oil ______	BEROAGM
4. Northern ______	HLGIST

CLUE: Assuming you've achieved this, it took you some time.

BONUS

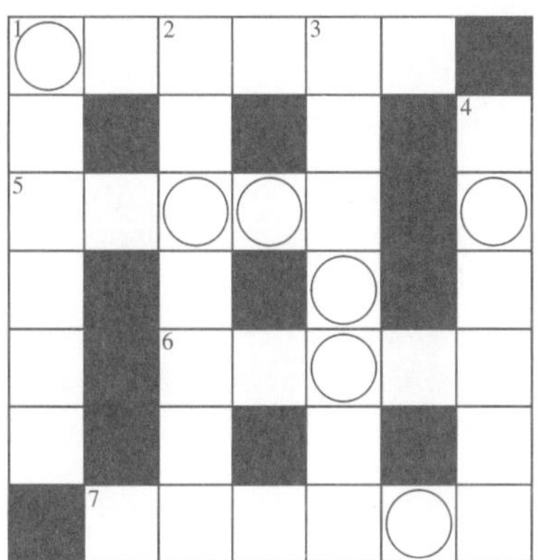

ACROSS

CLUE	ANSWER
1. Type of ape	BNOBIG
5. No ______	UDBOT
6. ______ Day	RIODS
7. Prepares	ROGSMO

DOWN

CLUE	ANSWER
1. Contraption	TDGGAE
2. Colorado city	UDEOBLR
3. London, ______	NIOTRAO
4. Dissertation	HITSES

CLUE: This European port city is home to almost 2 million people.

BONUS ◯◯◯◯◯◯◯

ACROSS

CLUE	ANSWER
1. ______ increase	LASRAY
5. Smith's movie machine	BOROT
6. 9,9,9	NNESI
7. Dangerous	FNASEU

DOWN

CLUE	ANSWER
1. ______ water	PIRSGN
2. A country	BOELNAN
3. Type of room	TRNUAOD
4. Foam substance	UMESSO

CLUE: Kid

BONUS

ACROSS

CLUE	ANSWER
1. _____ pie	RCEHYR
5. Accustomed	LUAUS
6. Same as stated	TIDOT
7. Swaps	RATSED

DOWN

CLUE	ANSWER
1. Pieces	HCKSUN
2. A country	UECDARO
3. Connected	LERTADE
4. Station _____	ANSWOG

BONUS

CLUE: This long-running show debuted on NBC in 1952.

ACROSS

CLUE	ANSWER
1. Uttered	KNPSOE
5. Foundation	BSSIA
6. ______ horizon	NVTEE
7. Type of injury	REHIAN

DOWN

CLUE	ANSWER
1. Surrounding area	USUBBR
2. Raunchy	BNOCSEE
3. ______ Europe	TSEARNE
4. Opposed to	ACROTN

CLUE: This debuted on store shelves in the 1940s.

BONUS ○○○○○○○○

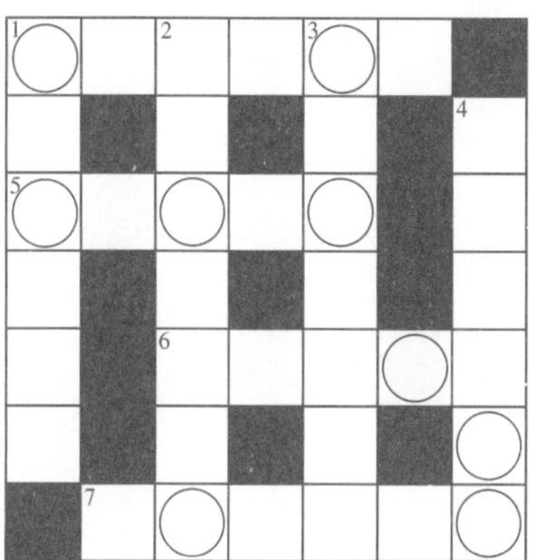

ACROSS

CLUE	ANSWER
1. Pulled	DUALEH
5. Expressive	LVAOC
6. Type of snake	PIVRE
7. Varney role	REESTN

DOWN

CLUE	ANSWER
1. Island city	AAHNAV
2. Reveal	NUOCREV
3. Surpass	LCEPIES
4. "Talkative" creature	TRARPO

CLUE: Louis ______ formed his car company in 1911.

BONUS ○○○○○○○○○

ACROSS

CLUE	ANSWER
1. ______ tree	ECYRRH
5. Drive	PMILE
6. Say	TRETU
7. ______ figures	NUECSS

DOWN

CLUE	ANSWER
1. Bells	HICSEM
2. Support	PUSEOES
3. Tells	LERTASE
4. A river	TISIRG

CLUE: The Greek goddess of divine retribution and vengeance

BONUS ◯◯◯◯◯◯◯

ACROSS

CLUE	ANSWER
1. Chaos	MMAEHY
5. Corn ______	YRSPU
6. Egyptian city	NSAAW
7. Almost	AENYLR

DOWN

CLUE	ANSWER
1. Art ______	UMESMU
2. Distance	RGEAYAD
3. Authorize	PMEWORE
4. ______ bean	DEINKY

CLUE: It is believed that this makes up about 8 percent of the Earth's crust.

BONUS 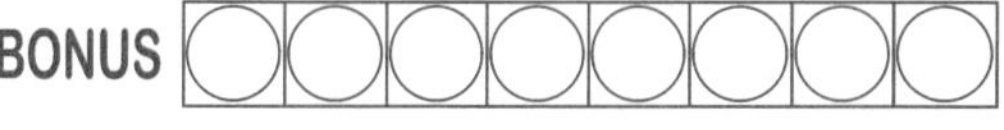

ACROSS

CLUE	ANSWER
1. Cut	DSLEIC
5. Populous country	NICHA
6. First Zodiac sign	RASIE
7. People	NBIESG

DOWN

CLUE	ANSWER
1. Part	EORSTC
2. Copy	MITAEIT
3. Tax ______	AISNOVE
4. Hand tops	RWITSS

BONUS

CLUE: The ______ ______ Company was the first to introduce the aluminum can.

ACROSS

CLUE	ANSWER
1. Grouped	REHDDE
5. ______ boom	NIOSC
6. Smarter	EIRSW
7. With pleasure	DYLLGA

DOWN

CLUE	ANSWER
1. Hurry	EHLUTS
2. Urban ______	AERLWEN
3. Absolved	XEUCDES
4. Commotion	LRUYRF

CLUE: Before starting a car company, this man worked for Westinghouse servicing steam engines.

BONUS  

JUMBLE® CrossWords™

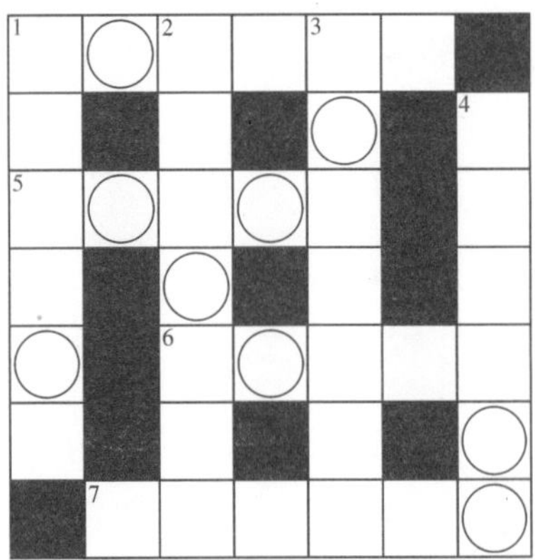

ACROSS

CLUE	ANSWER
1. Spot	TCNOIE
5. Good ______	RPTOS
6. Mythical hunter	NOOIR
7. Fatalities	TEDSHA

DOWN

CLUE	ANSWER
1. Island capital	USNSAA
2. Pair	WTSMOEO
3. Aromatic herb	TCIMTAN
4. Fails	LUFNSK

CLUE: In 1983, this woman was inducted into the Michigan Women's Hall of Fame for her achievements in civil rights.

BONUS  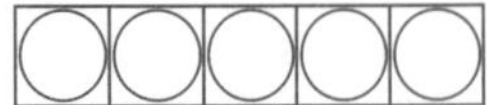

ACROSS

CLUE	ANSWER
1. Type of top	RJYEES
5. Hoarder of money	MREIS
6. ______ Hayes	AAISC
7. Defective	BKNERO

DOWN

CLUE	ANSWER
1. Mix up	EMJLBU
2. More hazardous	RRIEKIS
3. Designate	ARKERMA
4. Mexican resort	NNCUAC

BONUS **CLUE:** This man took up golf at the age of 10 and went on to win six Ohio State Junior titles.

ACROSS

CLUE	ANSWER
1. Swiped	NLOTSE
5. Feelings	BVSIE
6. Domain	MRLAE
7. Annul	PERLAE

DOWN

CLUE	ANSWER
1. Yummy	AYSOVR
2. Joan or Dave	BSOROEN
3. Entrap	NESANER
4. Beat soundly	LMPEMU

CLUE: James Gamble developed this in 1879.

BONUS 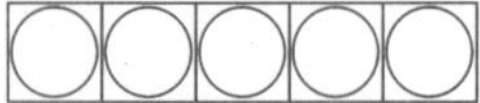 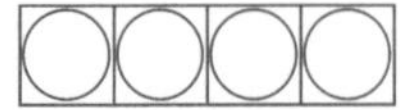

ACROSS

CLUE	ANSWER
1. ______ cabinet	FIGILN
5. A branch of philosophy	LCIOG
6. Type of tree	HEBCE
7. Top ______	TSEERC

DOWN

CLUE	ANSWER
1. Type of bird	AOLFNC
2. Understandable	LEELBIG
3. Atomic	NCRAUEL
4. Result	PHSTOU

BONUS

CLUE: This country has more than 10 official languages.

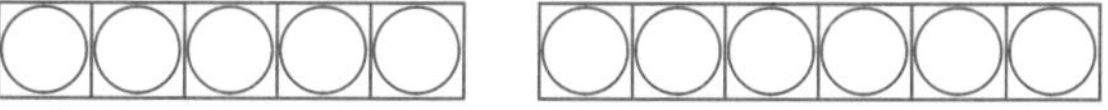

ACROSS

CLUE	ANSWER
1. Sordid	LZYSAE
5. ______ football	NRAAE
6. Precise	TECAX
7. Stuffy	DTGSOY

DOWN

CLUE	ANSWER
1. Ice ______	KSTASE
2. Mount ______	TESREEV
3. New ______	EDZNAAL
4. Gabby	HTYCAT

CLUE: This game is called draughts in England.

BONUS

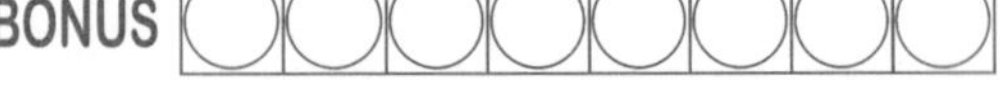

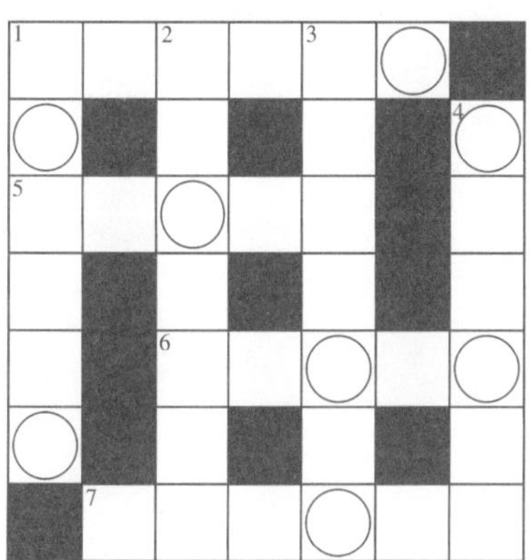

ACROSS

CLUE	ANSWER
1. Reason	TMEVIO
5. ______ Sea	HNTRO
6. Male relative	LNEUC
7. Flannel ______	HTESES

DOWN

CLUE	ANSWER
1. Type of insect	NAMSIT
2. Done	HRGTUOH
3. Car or truck	HELVIEC
4. Compulsory force	RUDSES

CLUE: Contract

BONUS

ACROSS

CLUE	ANSWER
1. ______ soda	NKABIG
5. ______ cake	YALRE
6. A form of oxygen	EONOZ
7. Powerlessly	KMYLEE

DOWN

CLUE	ANSWER
1. Left quickly	DBEOTL
2. ______ address	TEEKNOY
3. A U.S.city	RKONOFL
4. Avaricious	YRGEDE

CLUE: Contract

BONUS

ACROSS

CLUE	ANSWER
1. Detective	TLEHSU
5. Storage area	TCITA
6. Bad	WLUFA
7. Delays	TSLASL

DOWN

CLUE	ANSWER
1. Held in common	HSRADE
2. Take out	TXEARTC
3. Sensitive	LCTUATF
4. Planets	RWSDLO

BONUS **CLUE:** This actress played a singing and dancing mermaid on the *The Love Boat*

○○○○ ○○○○○○○

JUMBLE® CrossWords™

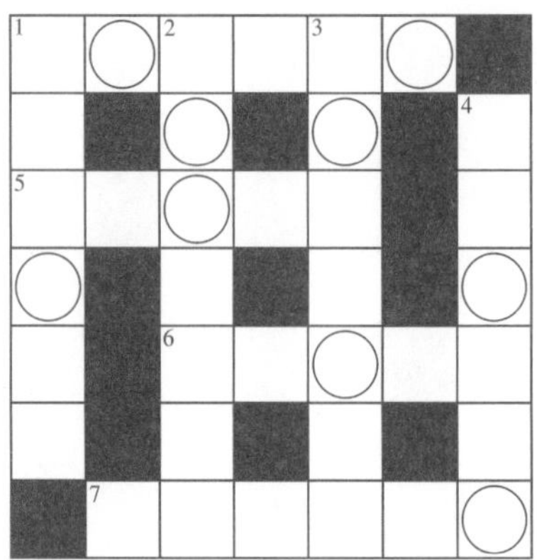

ACROSS

CLUE	ANSWER
1. Discarded	MDUPDE
5. Peter ______	LDEOY
6. Instruments	BOSEO
7. Divulge	LVRAEE

DOWN

CLUE	ANSWER
1. Eludes	DDGOSE
2. Type of post	PYAMLEO
3. Unattractive sight	ROSEYEE
4. Type of diplomat	LCONSU

BONUS **CLUE:** Miss

ACROSS

CLUE	ANSWER
1. ______ ticket	LAFREF
5. Oil ______	ANTIP
6. Mistreat	EBASU
7. ______ Irons	MREJYE

DOWN

CLUE	ANSWER
1. Special ______	PRTROE
2. Type of ship	RGIFAET
3. Leafy plant	ETCTLUE
4. Without restrictions	EREFYL

CLUE: This U.S. president invented the first hideaway bed ever patented in the United States.

BONUS 

ACROSS

CLUE	ANSWER
1. Drenched	DSEOKA
5. Competitor	RREAC
6. One of 50	DOHIA
7. Danson sitcom	BRCEEK

DOWN

CLUE	ANSWER
1. Jet ______	MARTSE
2. Attribute	EASBIRC
3. Appropriate	KREAAMR
4. ______ pool	NIODRO

CLUE: This was the first country to which the United States sent a woman as ambassador.

BONUS ◯◯◯◯◯◯◯

ACROSS

CLUE	ANSWER
1. Created	RMFDEO
5. Inspired	EUDGR
6. Perfectly suited	DILAE
7. Jane ______	TJNOSE

DOWN

CLUE	ANSWER
1. Battled	TUGOFH
2. Style of music	AMERITG
3. Ongoing	DSNEELS
4. Fiddle	NIOILV

CLUE: The "Pelican State"

BONUS ○○○○○○○○○

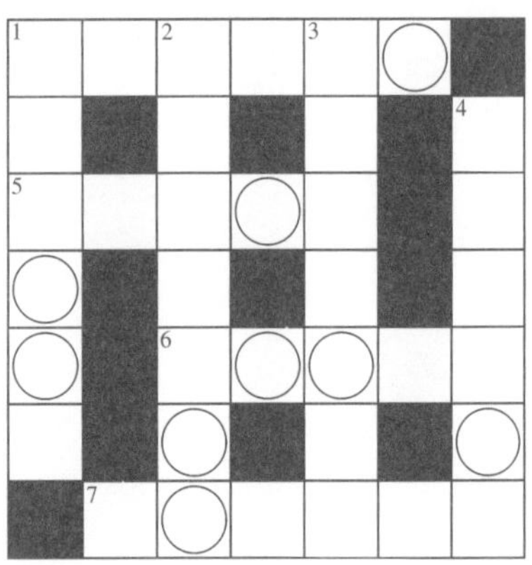

ACROSS

CLUE	ANSWER
1. Optimistic	PEBUTA
5. Horde	MWRAS
6. Playing pieces	NIKSG
7. Piles	TKSSCA

DOWN

CLUE	ANSWER
1. Consequence	PTSUOH
2. Beach ______	TLABKNE
3. Type of book	MCLANAA
4. Structures	HSOSEU

CLUE: The name for this part of the world is derived from a Latin verb meaning "to rise."

BONUS  

ACROSS

CLUE	ANSWER
1. Annually	LYERAY
5. Happening	TENEV
6. ______ coffee	RISIH
7. Venus, to Earth	MERAWR

DOWN

CLUE	ANSWER
1. Gives in	EIYDLS
2. Middle ______	MAIRAEC
3. Highly reactive metal	UTILIHM
4. ______ fluid	ASRWHE

BONUS **CLUE:** This newswoman won America's Junior Miss crown in 1963.

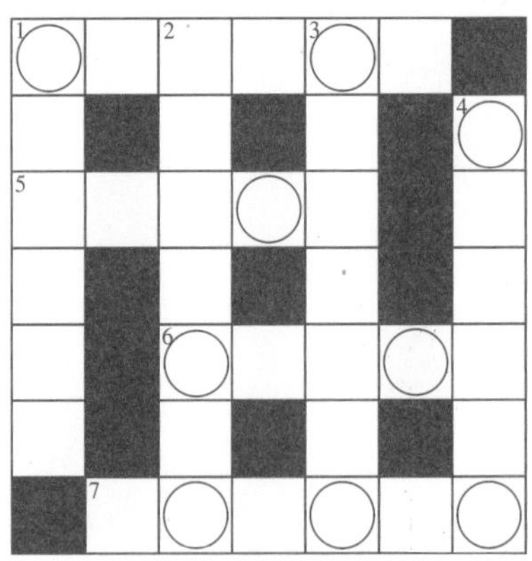

ACROSS

CLUE	ANSWER
1. Part of a car	DEENRF
5. Green ______	BHTMU
6. Rustic	RRLAU
7. Pessimistic	MLOGOY

DOWN

CLUE	ANSWER
1. ______ figure	RATFEH
2. "N"	LNAERUT
3. Oil ______	BMERAOG
4. Intercept unexpectedly	YAWYAL

CLUE: The official state flower of Massachusetts.

BONUS

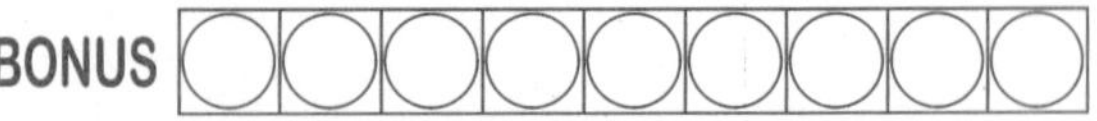

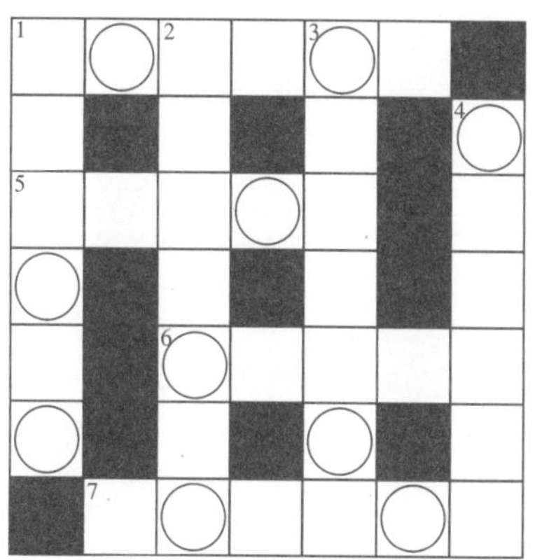

ACROSS

CLUE	ANSWER
1. Downhill ______	KRSSIE
5. Conference	RFMUO
6. Heavy block	NALIV
7. Type of bird	PRSOYE

DOWN

CLUE	ANSWER
1. Examined and sorted	FISTDE
2. Advancements	RNIAOSD
3. Spot ______	MEEROVR
4. Type of grain	RBYELA

CLUE: This car company produced a car called the Dictator from 1927–1937.

BONUS ○○○○○○○○○○

JUMBLE® CrossWords™

ACROSS

CLUE	ANSWER
1. _____ movie	RROOHR
5. Southern "chain"	DNASE
6. Crack up	MAESU
7. A European city	TANEHS

DOWN

CLUE	ANSWER
1. Break	AIHUTS
2. Beaming	TRANAID
3. Cloudy	BSOUCRE
4. Groups	FESTLE

BONUS

CLUE: Clark Gable died 11 days after this film was finished shooting.

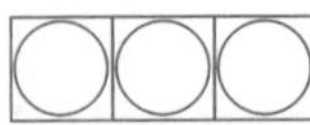

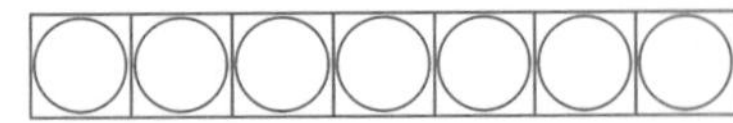

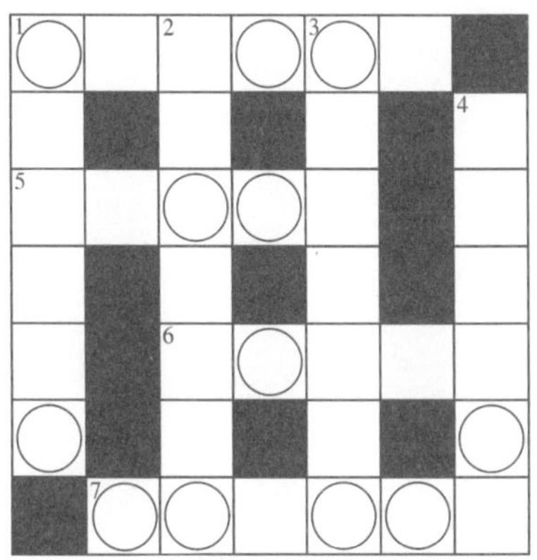

ACROSS

CLUE	ANSWER
1. ______ Lennon	LJIANU
5. A card game	MRUYM
6. Wear away	REDOE
7. Remained	TSYADE

DOWN

CLUE	ANSWER
1. A decision maker	UTJIRS
2. Jack ______	MLEBTRA
3. Some person	NABYYDO
4. Calculating	RHDSWE

CLUE: This actor achieved the rank of colonel in the Air Force and earned the Air Medal, the Distinguished Flying Cross, the Croix de Guerre, and 7 battle stars.

BONUS

ACROSS

CLUE	ANSWER
1. Understated	BTSULE
5. James ______	NAOSM
6. A bone	ERMUF
7. Smoothed	DNALEP

DOWN

CLUE	ANSWER
1. Representation	LMYSOB
2. Timid	USALBFH
3. Type of player	MENIANL
4. Hideous	DRIHOR

BONUS

CLUE: Harrison Ford film with Rutger Hauer and Sean Young.

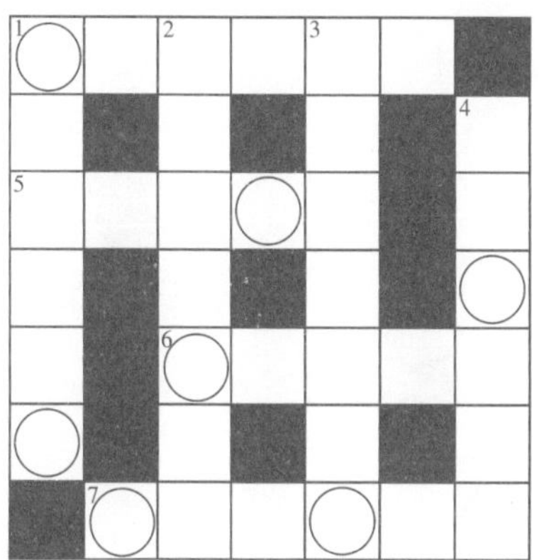

ACROSS

CLUE	ANSWER
1. Short, pointed weapon	ADREGG
5. Type of tooth	RMAOL
6. Easily understood	DLIUC
7. ______ club	MCYEDO

DOWN

CLUE	ANSWER
1. Moisten	PMAEDN
2. Historical Italian	LOAGLIE
3. Reason to see a doctor	REACAEH
4. The sixth of its kind	YFDIAR

CLUE: This country is home to about 200 volcanoes.

BONUS ○○○○○○○

ACROSS

CLUE	ANSWER
1. Humans	LOPEEP
5. Forbidden	BOATO
6. Educate	RIATN
7. Harness	BELRID

DOWN

CLUE	ANSWER
1. Customer	TOAPNR
2. Satellite	EROTIRB
3. Justin ______	LDREANO
4. Street	EEAUVN

CLUE: This is the only Middle Eastern country without a desert.

BONUS 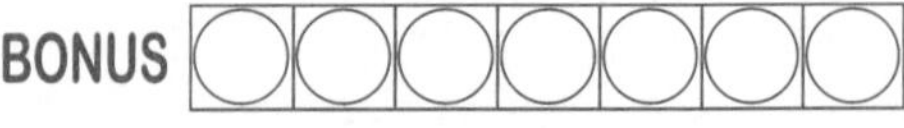

ACROSS

CLUE	ANSWER
1. Heritage	LCYEAG
5. A Ford or a horse	TNIOP
6. Mass of metal	NTOIG
7. Fixed	NEEMDD

DOWN

CLUE	ANSWER
1. ______ computer	PALPOT
2. Real	NNEGIUE
3. Congested	LGODCEG
4. Raised	FILDET

BONUS **CLUE:** This athlete was the only American to win a gold medal at the 1968 Winter Olympics.

JUMBLE® CrossWords™

ACROSS

CLUE	ANSWER
1. Trimmed	DSEHVA
5. White ______	RCIBH
6. Shoe ______	LSEAC
7. Climbed	DASECL

DOWN

CLUE	ANSWER
1. Cried	BSDEBO
2. A synthetic fabric	RCCIALY
3. Virtuous	THECILA
4. Ordered	DSBEOS

BONUS

CLUE: This actor was the first African American to win an Emmy award.

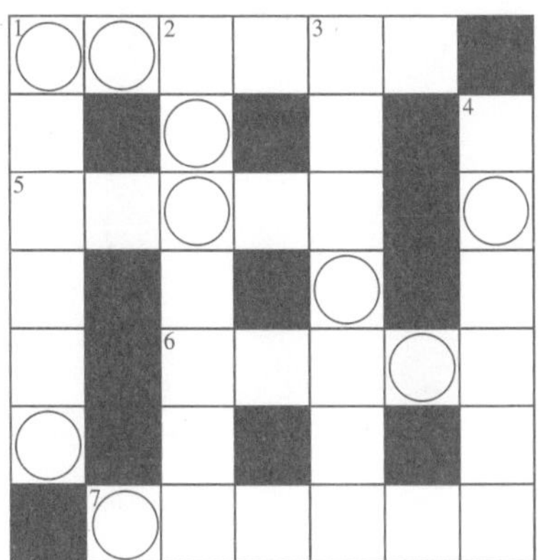

ACROSS

CLUE	ANSWER
1. Responds	ARESTC
5. All ______	LRCEA
6. An Eskimo language	NITUI
7. Crushes	MSSEAH

DOWN

CLUE	ANSWER
1. World ______	ECRDRO
2. Middle ______	REMAIAC
3. Done	TUGHHOR
4. Strong points	FSEOTR

BONUS **CLUE:** This actress's real name is Demetria Gene Guynes.

 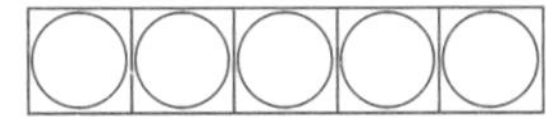

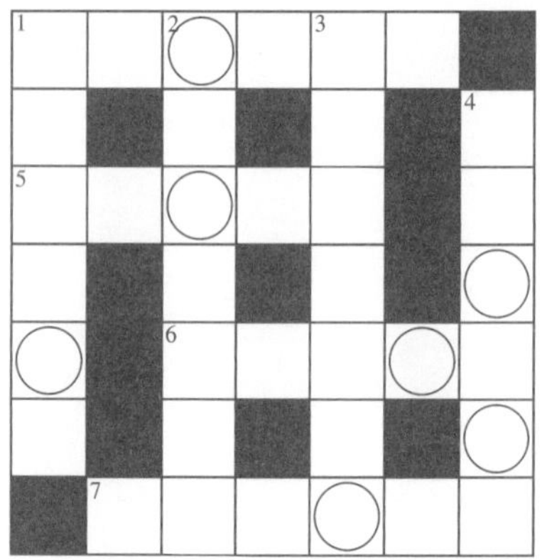

ACROSS

CLUE	ANSWER
1. Cruel	URBTLA
5. Bush	HSBUR
6. Vaughn or Carter	NIVEC
7. Constantly	LWSYAA

DOWN

CLUE	ANSWER
1. ______ case	EATBKS
2. Fall apart	LRENUVA
3. Home to Durrës	BILAAAN
4. Music ______	DEIVSO

CLUE: This country, which lies on the Equator, is home to the snow-capped volcanic peaks of Chimborazo (20,702 ft.) and Cotopaxi (19,347 ft.).

BONUS

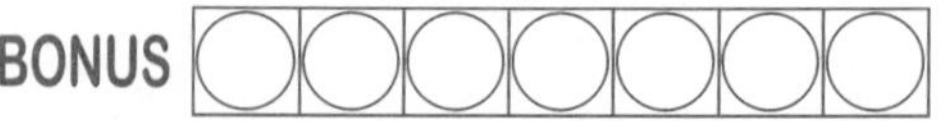

1	◯	2		3		■
	■	◯	■		■	4
5	◯				■	
	■		■	◯	■	◯
	■	6				◯
◯	■		■		■	
■	7			◯		

ACROSS

CLUE	ANSWER
1. Pocket _____	NAHEGC
5. Golden _____	ALEEG
6. _____ Hayes	ACISA
7. Hinder	HWTRAT

DOWN

CLUE	ANSWER
1. Winged infant	EHCBUR
2. Distress	NISAGUH
3. An island country	RAEGAND
4. Water _____	UAFTEC

CLUE: This man was the only U.S. president to remain a bachelor during his entire presidency.

BONUS 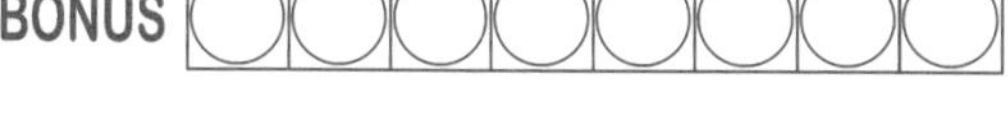

ACROSS

CLUE	ANSWER
1. ______ number	MROADN
5. Type of group	TCOET
6. The 24th of its kind	AOMGE
7. Abilities	LIKSSL

DOWN

CLUE	ANSWER
1. Protested violently	RDEITO
2. Television ______	TEKRNOW
3. ______ cookie	ATMOLEA
4. Badger	AHSSAR

CLUE: This is one of the most-visited homes in the United States.

BONUS ○○○○○○○○○

ACROSS

CLUE	ANSWER
1. Change	DYMIOF
5. Bacon or James	NKIEV
6. Extent	ACERH
7. Mailer	DRNESE

DOWN

CLUE	ANSWER
1. Creating	KGAMIN
2. Varied	EDSIREV
3. Home to Espoo	NDIFALN
4. Window ______	RWAEHS

BONUS **CLUE:** This adjustable tool was invented in the mid-1800s.

JUMBLE® CrossWords™

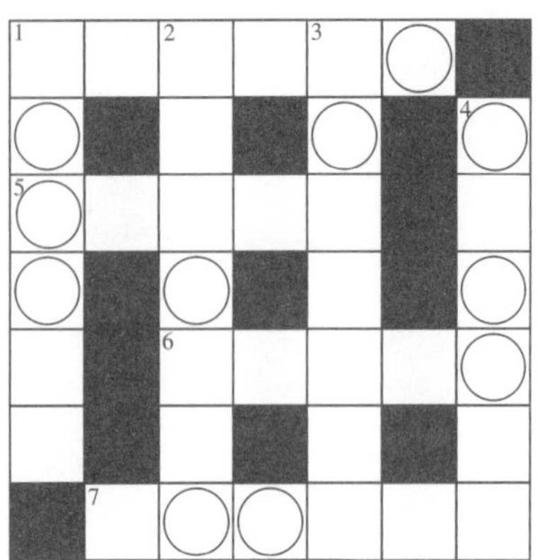

ACROSS

CLUE	ANSWER
1. Small	NIMEUT
5. Long Island _____	UDNOS
6. Jeremy _____	RISNO
7. Supposition	HIESTS

DOWN

CLUE	ANSWER
1. Concealed	AKDESM
2. Feed	HNOSIRU
3. Humdrum	TSEUIOD
4. Stages	HESPSA

BONUS

CLUE: This man was the first person, other than royalty, to appear on a British postage stamp.

ACROSS

CLUE	ANSWER
1. Ron ______	DHROAW
5. Area	AERML
6. Stockpile	DHROA
7. Granular	TIRYTG

DOWN

CLUE	ANSWER
1. Ed ______	RHASIR
2. The ______ Channel	REEHTAW
3. Widespread	MATNRPA
4. Scarcely	RAHYLD

CLUE: This is the only common, two-syllable word in the English language without an A, E, I, O, or U.

BONUS 

JUMBLE® CrossWords™

ACROSS

CLUE	ANSWER
1. The ______ (movie)	TAMXIR
5. Subdivisions	RATSP
6. Type of home	LOGIO
7. A result of an injury	HINSRE

DOWN

CLUE	ANSWER
1. *The ______ Movie*	TPUMEP
2. Befoul	RATINHS
3. A type of hormone	NSILIUN
4. ______ plumbing	DONIRO

CLUE: Carrie Fisher made her film debut in this 1975 movie.

BONUS 

ACROSS

CLUE	ANSWER
1. ______ acid	RITCIC
5. Merger	NNIOU
6. Rainbow ______	TRTUO
7. Formal	ESRDYS

DOWN

CLUE	ANSWER
1. Car or cat	UCRAGO
2. Type of storm	WTSIRET
3. Type of rock	NGIOESU
4. To a great extent	LAYVTS

BONUS **CLUE:** This man was the first guest host of *Saturday Night Live.*

◯◯◯◯◯◯ ◯◯◯◯◯◯

ACROSS

CLUE	ANSWER
1. A color	NIESAN
5. Leave	TPILS
6. Obvious	LINAP
7. Freshest	TNESEW

DOWN

CLUE	ANSWER
1. ______ seed	EMSEAS
2. Surpass	LCEPIES
3. Sodium ______	TINARET
4. ______ sauce	EPNATU

BONUS **CLUE:** This actor was the oldest driver in the 1979 LeMans 24-hour race.

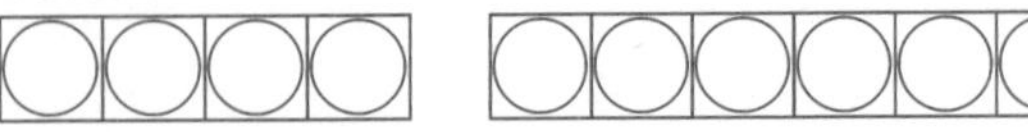

ACROSS

CLUE	ANSWER
1. Take back	EKEROV
5. Fleshy fruit	LMNOE
6. Government _____	NGTAE
7. Means	HTOEDM

DOWN

CLUE	ANSWER
1. Comment	MERKRA
2. Town	LGIVALE
3. _____ Cole	EENTNKH
4. Defeated badly	UORDET

BONUS

CLUE: This bird is the official state bird of New Mexico.

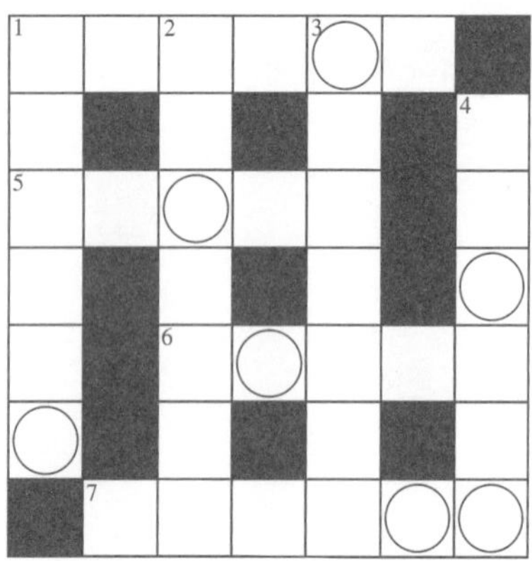

ACROSS

CLUE	ANSWER
1. ______ show	PTPEUP
5. Scrooge	RMIES
6. Say	ETURT
7. Light	NEOBCA

DOWN

CLUE	ANSWER
1. Excited	MPPUDE
2. Stance	PEROUST
3. Unpredictable	RARCITE
4. ______ Buffet	AWNRER

CLUE: With about 1,700 species, these are the largest order of mammal.

BONUS

ACROSS

CLUE	ANSWER
1. Bait	TNECIE
5. "B"	RBNOO
6. Red _____	LARET
7. Inn	TSEOLH

DOWN

CLUE	ANSWER
1. Set out	RMKEBA
2. Type of storm	ROTANOD
3. Link	TNCOCEN
4. _____ property	NERLAT

BONUS

CLUE: This animal has three toes on each foot.

JUMBLE® CrossWords™

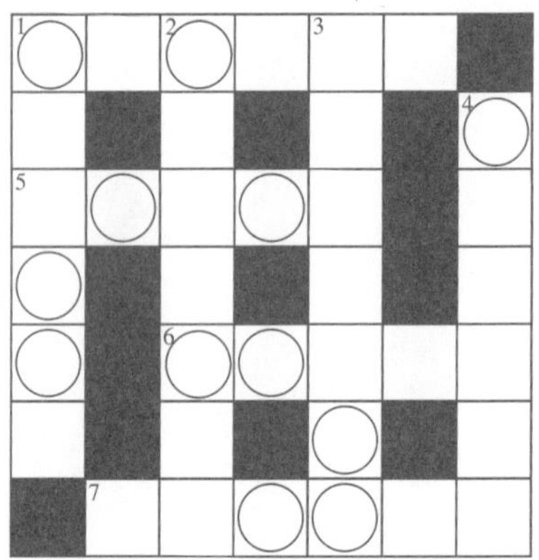

ACROSS

CLUE	ANSWER
1. Child classification	PONAHR
5. Pivots	RUTSN
6. ______ circle	NIREN
7. Piles	TKACSS

DOWN

CLUE	ANSWER
1. Fiber ______	POITSC
2. Prevail	PREISST
3. A poisonous element	RAESCIN
4. ______ wheel	FRESIR

BONUS **CLUE:** This company dates back to the 1860s.

ACROSS

CLUE	ANSWER
1. Aromatic resin	ALBMAS
5. ______ Manhattan	WOLRE
6. European ______	NUNIO
7. Sea ______	TOETSR

DOWN

CLUE	ANSWER
1. ______ box	TLBOAL
2. Type of case	WIALSUT
3. ______ ticket	RIAILEN
4. Mixes	NELSDB

CLUE: Traditionally, strawberries and cream are served at this annual sporting event.

BONUS 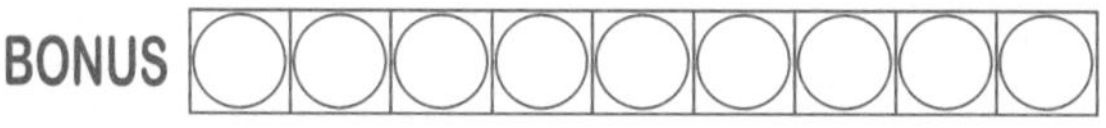

JUMBLE® CrossWords™

ACROSS

CLUE	ANSWER
1. ______ hat	NAPAAM
5. Energy	RVIOG
6. Authorize	AENTC
7. Dull	DOTSYG

DOWN

CLUE	ANSWER
1. A dog owner	VOVALP
2. Disregard	ECTNELG
3. Mythical female	RMAMIDE
4. Guard	TENSRY

CLUE: As of 2005, this city was the most-populous city south of the Equator.

BONUS

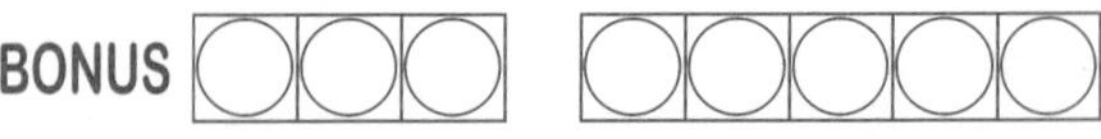

ACROSS

CLUE	ANSWER
1. Acquired	NIAGDE
5. Stallone role	ARMOB
6. Commotion	NIESO
7. Bushes	DEHSEG

DOWN

CLUE	ANSWER
1. Type of belt	RGRETA
2. Large	MIEMESN
3. Stimulating	NVGEIOK
4. Many	ZODSNE

CLUE: More than 200 islands are part of this region.

BONUS

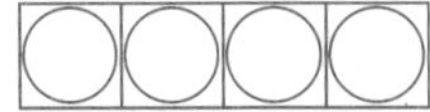

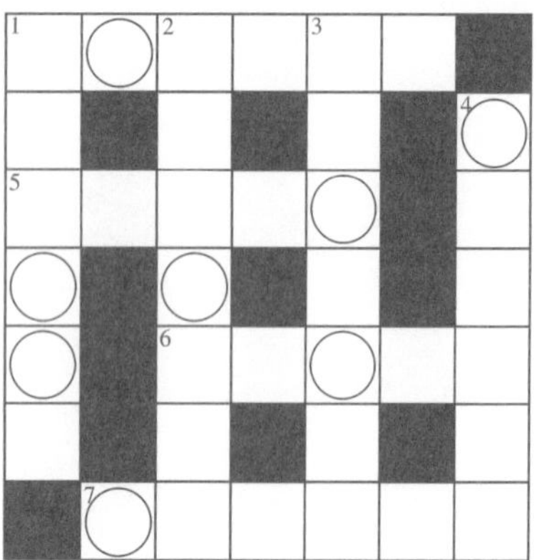

ACROSS

CLUE	ANSWER
1. A predatory insect	AISMTN
5. Type of boat	YTHAC
6. Display	DXUEE
7. Welcomes	REGSTE

DOWN

CLUE	ANSWER
1. Leaders	YMSROA
2. ______ reaction	NRAUELC
3. Trespass	TNIURED
4. Grippers	LPEISR

CLUE: In 1755, an earthquake killed more than 30,000 people in this country.

BONUS ◯◯◯◯◯◯◯◯

ACROSS

CLUE	ANSWER
1. Large bird	NCROOD
5. Hung loosely	LNUSG
6. Clean off	NIRES
7. Pants	AKLCSS

DOWN

CLUE	ANSWER
1. Type of nut	AEWCHS
2. "N"	ELUNRTA
3. Natural	RIGCOAN
4. European city	HTASNE

CLUE: This was named after English physician Sir Joseph Lister who performed the first antiseptic surgery in 1865.

BONUS 

JUMBLE® CrossWords™

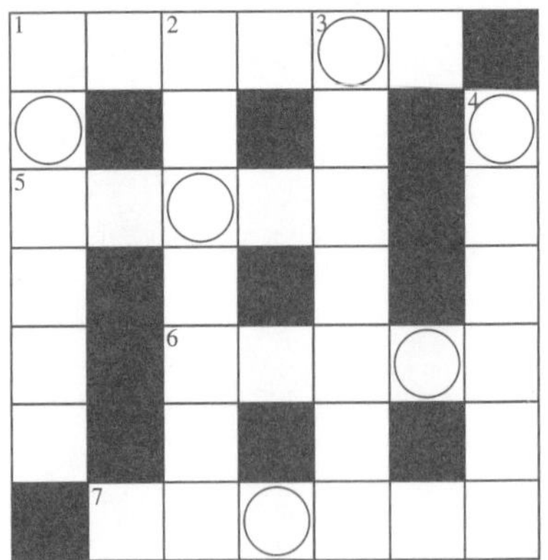

ACROSS

CLUE	ANSWER
1. Type of reptile	AINGAU
5. Rift	MCSAH
6. Asian country	NIAID
7. Responds	ATRECS

DOWN

CLUE	ANSWER
1. Needed scratching	TCIDEH
2. Different	NULAEIK
3. Roaming	MIOCNDA
4. Destroys	RKWAES

CLUE: This island has one of the highest population densities in the world.

BONUS 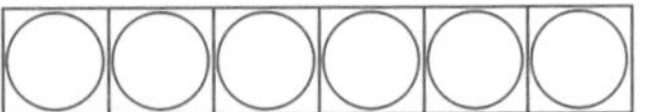

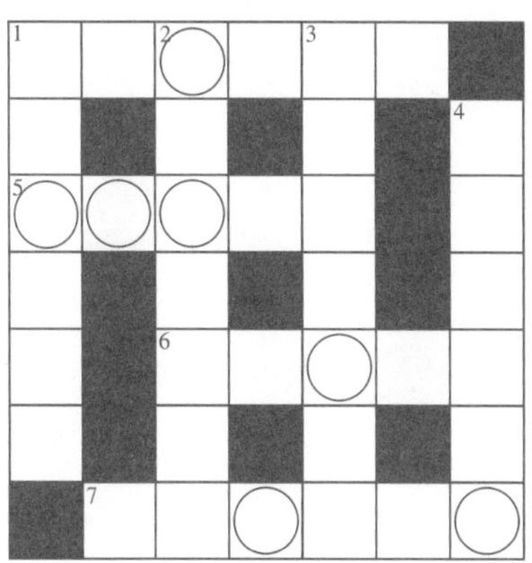

ACROSS

CLUE	ANSWER
1. Indentation	EECRSS
5. Exceeding number	AOVEB
6. Same as	TOTID
7. Footprints	ARTSKC

DOWN

CLUE	ANSWER
1. Cooks	SRTSOA
2. Seafood ______	ERDOCHW
3. Doubter	PEKSCIT
4. Teachers	USRTTO

CLUE: This sauce was named after a Mexican state.

BONUS ◯◯◯◯◯◯◯

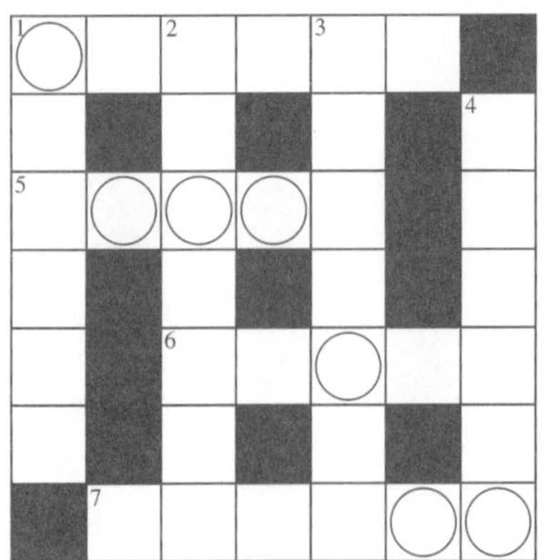

ACROSS

CLUE	ANSWER
1. Later's time	TFREUU
5. Loud metallic sound	GLCAN
6. Whoosh	SSWHI
7. Be present at	TDETNA

DOWN

CLUE	ANSWER
1. Looking toward	NFGAIC
2. Travel	ATSNRIT
3. Musical style	EGARITM
4. Flower type	DICHRO

CLUE: This country is home to approximately 200,000 lakes and 180,000 islands.

BONUS

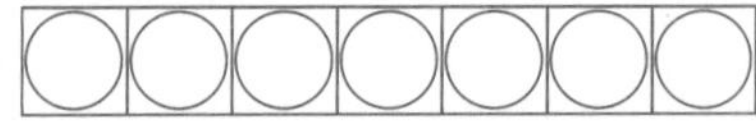

ACROSS

CLUE	ANSWER
1. Short spasm	ZSEEEN
5. ______, NE	AAHMO
6. A country	LYAIT
7. Peddler	DORNEV

DOWN

CLUE	ANSWER
1. Rocks	ENSOTS
2. Elusive	SAVEIEV
3. New ______	AEZLDNA
4. Trial ______	ALREWY

CLUE: After this man's presidency, he retired to his 230-acre farm near Gettysburg where he wrote his memoirs.

BONUS 

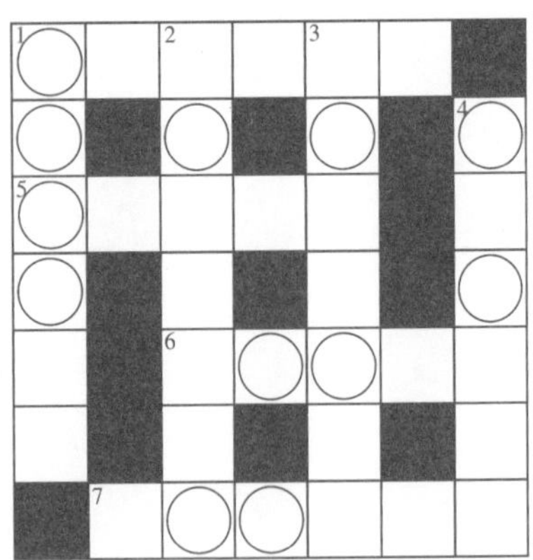

ACROSS

CLUE	ANSWER
1. Scoffed	RJDEEE
5. Fibbing	GLNIY
6. Wear away	ROEED
7. Stagnation	AITSSS

DOWN

CLUE	ANSWER
1. Shocked	DJEOTL
2. Clear	TNVIEDE
3. Captivate	GNOSRSE
4. A large city	NTSAEH

BONUS **CLUE:** At age six, this actor took dancing lessons from Fred Kelly, Gene Kelly's brother.

ACROSS

CLUE	ANSWER
1. Muscles	BPIESC
5. Confuse	PSMUT
6. ______ music	APKOL
7. To be sorry for	GETRER

DOWN

CLUE	ANSWER
1. Dark rock	AALTSB
2. Press into wrinkles	PRECUML
3. Widely accepted	URALPOP
4. Foil	WTAHTR

CLUE: Some ______ can grow to more than 80 feet in length.

BONUS ◯◯◯◯◯◯◯◯◯

ACROSS

CLUE	ANSWER
1. Petty	TRPYLA
5. Lure	MTTEP
6. ______ Mountains	RAKZO
7. ______ pine	KYTONT

DOWN

CLUE	ANSWER
1. Foul	UITRDP
2. Satire	NMALOOP
3. Withdraw	TCETRRA
4. ______ business	NYOMEK

BONUS

CLUE: Idiot

ACROSS

CLUE	ANSWER
1. Wild canine	ACJLAK
5. Country-like	RRLAU
6. Obeys	SDIMN
7. Bodies of water	ASCEON

DOWN

CLUE	ANSWER
1. New _____	YSEREJ
2. Pottery classification	RECCIAM
3. A U.S.city	TLNAAAT
4. Believes in	UTSRST

CLUE: In 1972, Ceylon changed its name to this.

BONUS ◯◯◯ ◯◯◯◯◯

JUMBLE® CrossWords™

ACROSS

CLUE	ANSWER
1. Overwhelming amount	LUEEDG
5. Chocolate-brown color	AOHCM
6. Move slightly	DGEUN
7. An aunt or niece	LFEEAM

DOWN

CLUE	ANSWER
1. Territory	MODIAN
2. Permission	LCEENIS
3. Male relative	NARGAPD
4. Garment part	EEEVLS

CLUE: This U.S. president, with the help of his wife, was the first president to establish a permanent library in the White House.

BONUS ○○○○○○○○

ACROSS

CLUE	ANSWER
1. Disagreeable	KCNARY
5. Unstable	YRKCO
6. Release	TNEIU
7. Division of a poem	NATSAZ

DOWN

CLUE	ANSWER
1. Cerebral ______	ROCXTE
2. Explanation	NATCOUC
3. C. K.'s birthplace	TOKYPNR
4. Theater	MNCIAE

CLUE: This term means "empty orchestra" in Japanese.

BONUS

ACROSS

CLUE	ANSWER
1. Composite picture	MCIOAS
5. Revel selfishly	TGAOL
6. Home to Île de la Cité	RPSAI
7. Constructed	DFROEM

DOWN

CLUE	ANSWER
1. TV detective	AGMMUN
2. Zodiac sign	SOIORCP
3. Interval	TNIREIM
4. Mistreated	BEADSU

CLUE: This animal, which can weigh up to 1,600 pounds, can run on ice at speeds up to 25 miles per hour.

BONUS 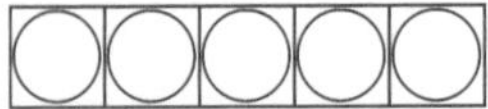 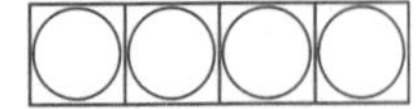

ACROSS

CLUE	ANSWER
1. ______ tax	MICONE
5. Fight	SJUOT
6. Celebration	RATYP
7. Seller	RDNOEV

DOWN

CLUE	ANSWER
1. Introduce forcefully	NCEJIT
2. Press into wrinkles	PRECUML
3. Aged	REUMDTA
4. Trial ______	ALREWY

CLUE: This U.S. president said, "America did not invent human rights. In a very real sense, it is the other way round. Human rights invented America."

BONUS

JUMBLE® CrossWords™

ACROSS

CLUE	ANSWER
1. Oblong box	FICNOF
5. Save	DAHOR
6. Produce with skill	TAFCR
7. Carrot, plum	WERRAD

DOWN

CLUE	ANSWER
1. Stick together	HORECE
2. Engaged woman	FENCIEA
3. One of 50	DINIAAN
4. Shocked	DJEOTL

CLUE: This actor, who was born in Oklahoma in 1954, appeared in his first film at the age of 18 months.

BONUS

ACROSS

CLUE	ANSWER
1. Imperfection	TLOHBC
5. Boiled candy	YFTFA
6. Sign up	TENRE
7. Fine plaster	CUTSOC

DOWN

CLUE	ANSWER
1. Annoy	HOTBRE
2. Quirky	TFOBFAE
3. Mysterious	RITYCPC
4. Coiffure	OHDAIR

CLUE: It takes about eight hours to drive here from New York City.

BONUS

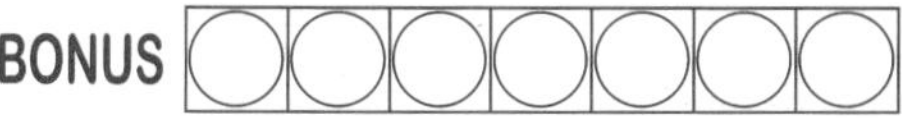

JUMBLE® CrossWords™

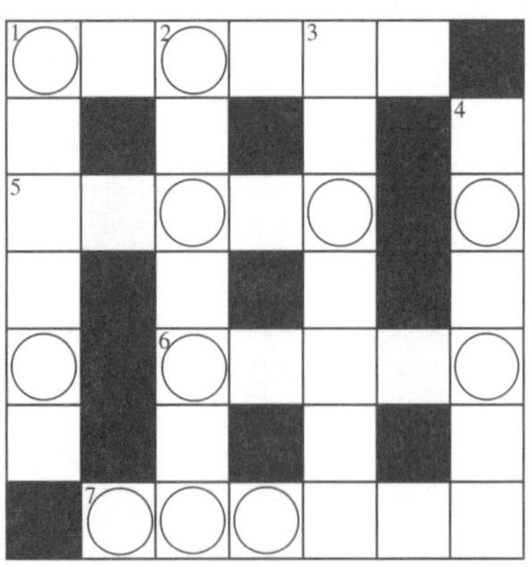

ACROSS

CLUE	ANSWER
1. Overpower	BSUDEU
5. Group of animals	KOFCL
6. Speed	PMOTE
7. Free	GSIRTA

DOWN

CLUE	ANSWER
1. Expedition	FSAAIR
2. ______ shot	RBEOSOT
3. Disorganized	KUENTPM
4. Fires	HTSOSO

CLUE: This music superstar, who went to Oklahoma State University on a partial athletic scholarship, threw the javelin on the track and field team.

BONUS

ACROSS

CLUE	ANSWER
1. Toe swelling	NNOIUB
5. Flyers	TKIES
6. Musical word	LCIRY
7. Beat	FTDAEE

DOWN

CLUE	ANSWER
1. Cookie factory	EAYKBR
2. ______ Wood	AALTNEI
3. Watch	BRESEOV
4. Variety of lynx	CBATOB

CLUE: This enduring host was inducted into the Academy of Television Arts & Sciences Hall of Fame in May 2004.

BONUS

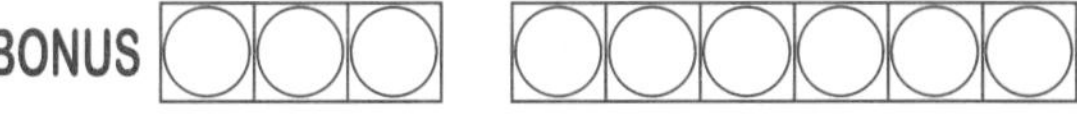

ACROSS

CLUE	ANSWER
1. Eliminate	MEREOV
5. Nervous	SEENT
6. ______ water	OCTIN
7. Wrongdoings	RCESIM

DOWN

CLUE	ANSWER
1. Allot	TRAINO
2. Tropical lizard	NOROIMT
3. A country	EITVMAN
4. Pants	ALSKCS

BONUS **CLUE:** Billions of these have been sold since their introduction in 1912.

pocket posh® JUMBLE® CrossWords™ 5

SOLUTIONS

1 1A-SCHEME 5A-SIMON 6A-THORN 7A-URANUS 1D-SESAME 2D-HAMSTER 3D-MONSOON 4D-EVENTS B-MINERVA

2 1A-EXPAND 5A-CHOIR 6A-UNION 7A-STAGES 1D-ESCAPE 2D-PRODUCT 3D-NURSING 4D-HAUNTS B-PHOENIX

3 1A-SUNDAY 5A-TOTEM 6A-BANJO 7A-PENCIL 1D-SETTER 2D-NOTABLE 3D-ALMANAC 4D-SCHOOL B-CARLY SIMON

4 1A-WEASEL 5A-MONTH 6A-YOUTH 7A-EDITOR 1D-WOMBAT 2D-ANNOYED 3D-EXHAUST 4D-RICHER B-CANTON, OHIO (FOOTBALL)

5 1A-AUSTIN 5A-GRASP 6A-UPSET 7A-ULCERS 1D-ANGERS 2D-SEAGULL 3D-IMPASSE 4D-CACTUS B-ANTARCTICA

6 1A-VERMIN 5A-KAPUT 6A-INNER 7A-DECENT 1D-VIKING 2D-REPTILE 3D-INTENSE 4D-SPIRIT B-SNICKERS

7 1A-MONKEY 5A-CLEAR 6A-FLASH 7A-FLAKES 1D-MICKEY 2D-NEEDFUL 3D-EARMARK 4D-EIGHTS B-MICHIGAN

8 1A-WISELY 5A-TARDY 6A-GOLLY 7A-STAYED 1D-WITTED 2D-SPRIGHT 3D-LOYALTY 4D-BUOYED B-HOWDY DOODY

9 1A-PETITE 5A-BREAD 6A-THORN 7A-GENEVA 1D-PUBLIC 2D-TRESTLE 3D-TADPOLE 4D-CORNEA B-PIERCE BROSNAN

10 1A-BUDDHA 5A-VAPOR 6A-OOZED 7A-KERNEL 1D-BOVINE 2D-DEPLORE 3D-HORIZON 4D-SANDAL B-HUDSON RIVER

11 1A-CARPET 5A-TULIP 6A-ERROL 7A-WELDER 1D-CATNIP 2D-RELIEVE 3D-EXPIRED 4D-FULLER B-TUPPERWARE

12 1A-BEYOND 5A-STRIP 6A-AMUSE 7A-DELETE 1D-BASALT 2D-YARDAGE 3D-NEPTUNE 4D-IMPEDE B-PILLSBURY

13 1A-FEEBLE 5A-CLIMB 6A-TORCH 7A-EDWARD 1D-FACING 2D-EVICTED 3D-LIBERIA 4D-INCHED B-IN THE OCEAN

14 1A-GRADED 5A-GIFTS 6A-INNER 7A-STRESS 1D-GIGGLE 2D-AFFLICT 3D-ESSENCE 4D-TAURUS B-FRED ASTAIRE

15 1A-BANDIT 5A-BRIEF 6A-HINGE 7A-CRAYON 1D-BABBLE 2D-NEITHER 3D-INFANCY 4D-SCREEN B-BIRTHDAYS

16 1A-RIGGED 5A-FLOOR 6A-GATES 7A-CANCEL 1D-RAFFLE 2D-GEORGIA 3D-ERRATIC 4D-VESSEL B-VELCRO

17 1A-ASPECT 5A-TAROT 6A-OLIVE 7A-METHOD 1D-ATTACK 2D-PURPOSE 3D-CATFISH 4D-SHIELD B-KOOL-AID

18 1A-MICRON 5A-INPUT 6A-IDEAL 7A-SEALED 1D-MAILED 2D-CAPTIVE 3D-OATMEAL 4D-NAILED B-LIAM NEESON

19 1A-NOTIFY 5A-VENOM 6A-GULFS 7A-STODGY 1D-NOVICE 2D-TONIGHT 3D-FUMBLED 4D-FRISKY B-MOCKINGBIRD

20 1A-CONRAD 5A-SIREN 6A-ABYSS 7A-HANDLE 1D-COSMIC 2D-NIRVANA 3D-ANNOYED 4D-LASSIE B-HONDA CIVIC

21 1A-THOMAS 5A-RUFUS 6A-NINTH 7A-TELLER 1D-TURTLE 2D-OFFENSE 3D-ARSENAL 4D-ANCHOR B-TENNESSEE

22 1A-MORGAN 5A-THUMB 6A-INNER 7A-SENATE 1D-METHOD 2D-ROUTINE 3D-ALBANIA 4D-HEARSE B-TORTOISE

23 1A-NUCLEUS 5A-SEIZE 6A-KOALA 7A-SINCERE 1D-NESTLES 2D-CHICKEN 3D-ELEVATE 4D-STORAGE B-STAR TREK

24 1A-ECLAIR 5A-STUMP 6A-DROVE 7A-ARREST 1D-EASILY 2D-LAUNDER 3D-IMPLORE 4D-HONEST B-VEHICLES

25 1A-DAMAGE 5A-DINER 6A-RUGBY 7A-CHOSEN 1D-DODGED 2D-MONARCH 3D-GARAGES 4D-BUNYAN B-BERMUDA

26 1A-CHUNKY 5A-DERBY 6A-VOTER 7A-CLONES 1D-CEDARS 2D-UNRAVEL 3D-KRYPTON 4D-STARTS B-BETTY CROCKER

27 1A-MAMMAL 5A-SALEM 6A-INNER 7A-BEACON 1D-MUSKET 2D-MALAISE 3D-ALMANAC 4D-PATRON B-BISMARCK

28 1A-METRIC 5A-SPANS 6A-LEEKS 7A-WRITES 1D-MISSED 2D-TRAILER 3D-INSPECT 4D-CEASES B-DENMARK

29 1A-SCREWY 5A-NOBEL 6A-RACES 7A-RHYTHM 1D-SANELY 2D-REBIRTH 3D-WILDCAT 4D-BALSAM B-BERLIN WALL

30 1A-DEPICT 5A-RAYON 6A-ERROR 7A-STOLEN 1D-DIRECT 2D-PAYMENT 3D-CONTROL 4D-MICRON B-ENCYCLOPEDIAS

31 1A-SUNDRY 5A-RUGBY 6A-RHODA 7A-PARDON 1D-STREAK 2D-NIGERIA 3D-RAYMOND 4D-OBTAIN B-HUNKY-DORY

32 1A-LOCKED 5A-SHRUB 6A-NORTH 7A-ACROSS 1D-LISTED 2D-CHRONIC 3D-EMBARGO 4D-LIGHTS B-ADULTHOOD

33 1A-GIBBON 5A-DOUBT 6A-DORIS 7A-GROOMS 1D-GADGET 2D-BOULDER 3D-ONTARIO 4D-THESIS B-HAMBURG

34 1A-SALARY 5A-ROBOT 6A-NINES 7A-UNSAFE 1D-SPRING 2D-LEBANON 3D-ROTUNDA 4D-MOUSSE B-YOUNGSTER

35 1A-CHERRY 5A-USUAL 6A-DITTO 7A-TRADES 1D-CHUNKS 2D-ECUADOR 3D-RELATED 4D-WAGONS B-THE TODAY SHOW

36 1A-SPOKEN 5A-BASIS 6A-EVENT 7A-HERNIA 1D-SUBURB 2D-OBSCENE 3D-EASTERN 4D-CONTRA B-CHEERIOS

37 1A-HAULED 5A-VOCAL 6A-VIPER 7A-ERNEST 1D-HAVANA 2D-UNCOVER 3D-ECLIPSE 4D-PARROT B-CHEVROLET

38 1A-CHERRY 5A-IMPEL 6A-UTTER 7A-CENSUS 1D-CHIMES 2D-ESPOUSE 3D-RELATES 4D-TIGRIS B-NEMESIS

39 1A-MAYHEM 5A-SYRUP 6A-ASWAN 7A-NEARLY 1D-MUSEUM 2D-YARDAGE 3D-EMPOWER 4D-KIDNEY B-ALUMINUM

40 1A-SLICED 5A-CHINA 6A-ARIES 7A-BEINGS 1D-SECTOR 2D-IMITATE 3D-EVASION 4D-WRISTS B-COORS BREWING

41 1A-HERDED 5A-SONIC 6A-WISER 7A-GLADLY 1D-HUSTLE 2D-RENEWAL 3D-EXCUSED 4D-FLURRY B-HENRY FORD

42 1A-NOTICE 5A-SPORT 6A-ORION 7A-DEATHS 1D-NASSAU 2D-TWOSOME 3D-CATMINT 4D-FLUNKS B-ROSA PARKS

43 1A-JERSEY 5A-MISER 6A-ISAAC 7A-BROKEN 1D-JUMBLE 2D-RISKIER 3D-EARMARK 4D-CANCUN B-JACK NICKLAUS

44 1A-STOLEN 5A-VIBES 6A-REALM 7A-REPEAL 1D-SAVORY 2D-OSBORNE 3D-ENSNARE 4D-PUMMEL B-IVORY SOAP

45 1A-FILING 5A-LOGIC 6A-BEECH 7A-SECRET 1D-FALCON 2D-LEGIBLE 3D-NUCLEAR 4D-UPSHOT B-SOUTH AFRICA

46 1A-SLEAZY 5A-ARENA 6A-EXACT 7A-STODGY 1D-SKATES 2D-EVEREST 3D-ZEALAND 4D-CHATTY B-CHECKERS

47 1A-MOTIVE 5A-NORTH 6A-UNCLE 7A-SHEETS 1D-MANTIS 2D-THROUGH 3D-VEHICLE 4D-DURESS B-DECREASE

48 1A-BAKING 5A-LAYER 6A-OZONE 7A-MEEKLY 1D-BOLTED 2D-KEYNOTE 3D-NORFOLK 4D-GREEDY B-AGREEMENT

49 1A-SLEUTH 5A-ATTIC 6A-AWFUL 7A-STALLS 1D-SHARED 2D-EXTRACT 3D-TACTFUL 4D-WORLDS B-TERI HATCHER

50 1A-DUMPED 5A-DOYLE 6A-OBOES 7A-REVEAL 1D-DODGES 2D-MAYPOLE 3D-EYESORE 4D-CONSUL B-YOUNG LADY

51 1A-RAFFLE 5A-PAINT 6A-ABUSE 7A-JEREMY 1D-REPORT 2D-FRIGATE 3D-LETTUCE 4D-FREELY B-JEFFERSON

52 1A-SOAKED 5A-RACER 6A-IDAHO 7A-BECKER 1D-STREAM 2D-ASCRIBE 3D-EARMARK 4D-INDOOR B-DENMARK

53 1A-FORMED 5A-URGED 6A-IDEAL 7A-JETSON 1D-FOUGHT 2D-RAGTIME 3D-ENDLESS 4D-VIOLIN B-LOUISIANA

54 1A-UPBEAT 5A-SWARM 6A-KINGS 7A-STACKS 1D-UPSHOT 2D-BLANKET 3D-ALMANAC 4D-HOUSES B-THE ORIENT

55 1A-YEARLY 5A-EVENT 6A-IRISH 7A-WARMER 1D-YIELDS 2D-AMERICA 3D-LITHIUM 4D-WASHER B-DIANE SAWYER

56 1A-FENDER 5A-THUMB 6A-RURAL 7A-GLOOMY 1D-FATHER 2D-NEUTRAL 3D-EMBARGO 4D-WAYLAY B-MAYFLOWER

57 1A-SKIERS 5A-FORUM 6A-ANVIL 7A-OSPREY 1D-SIFTED 2D-INROADS 3D-REMOVER 4D-BARLEY B-STUDEBAKER

58 1A-HORROR 5A-ANDES 6A-AMUSE 7A-ATHENS 1D-HIATUS 2D-RADIANT 3D-OBSCURE 4D-FLEETS B-THE MISFITS

59 1A-JULIAN 5A-RUMMY 6A-ERODE 7A-STAYED 1D-JURIST 2D-LAMBERT 3D-ANYBODY 4D-SHREWD B-JIMMY STEWART

60 1A-SUBTLE 5A-MASON 6A-FEMUR 7A-PLANED 1D-SYMBOL 2D-BASHFUL 3D-LINEMAN 4D-HORRID B-BLADE RUNNER

61 1A-DAGGER 5A-MOLAR 6A-LUCID 7A-COMEDY 1D-DAMPEN 2D-GALILEO 3D-EARACHE 4D-FRIDAY B-ICELAND

62 1A-PEOPLE 5A-TABOO 6A-TRAIN 7A-BRIDLE 1D-PATRON 2D-ORBITER 3D-LEONARD 4D-AVENUE B-LEBANON

63 1A-LEGACY 5A-PINTO 6A-INGOT 7A-MENDED 1D-LAPTOP 2D-GENUINE 3D-CLOGGED 4D-LIFTED B-PEGGY FLEMING

64 1A-SHAVED 5A-BIRCH 6A-LACES 7A-SCALED 1D-SOBBED 2D-ACRYLIC 3D-ETHICAL 4D-BOSSED B-BILL COSBY

65 1A-REACTS 5A-CLEAR 6A-INUIT 7A-MASHES 1D-RECORD 2D-AMERICA 3D-THROUGH 4D-FORTES B-DEMI MOORE

66 1A-BRUTAL 5A-SHRUB 6A-VINCE 7A-ALWAYS 1D-BASKET 2D-UNRAVEL 3D-ALBANIA 4D-VIDEOS B-ECUADOR

67 1A-CHANGE 5A-EAGLE 6A-ISAAC 7A-THWART 1D-CHERUB 2D-ANGUISH 3D-GRENADA 4D-FAUCET B-BUCHANAN

68 1A-RANDOM 5A-OCTET 6A-OMEGA 7A-SKILLS 1D-RIOTED 2D-NETWORK 3D-OATMEAL 4D-HARASS B-GRACELAND

69 1A-MODIFY 5A-KEVIN 6A-REACH 7A-SENDER 1D-MAKING 2D-DIVERSE 3D-FINLAND 4D-WASHER B-MONKEY WRENCH

70 1A-MINUTE 5A-SOUND 6A-IRONS 7A-THESIS 1D-MASKED 2D-NOURISH 3D-TEDIOUS 4D-PHASES B-SHAKESPEARE

71 1A-HOWARD 5A-REALM 6A-HOARD 7A-GRITTY 1D-HARRIS 2D-WEATHER 3D-RAMPANT 4D-HARDLY B-RHYTHM

72 1A-MATRIX 5A-PARTS 6A-IGLOO 7A-SHINER 1D-MUPPET 2D-TARNISH 3D-INSULIN 4D-INDOOR B-SHAMPOO

73 1A-CITRIC 5A-UNION 6A-TROUT 7A-DRESSY 1D-COUGAR 2D-TWISTER 3D-IGNEOUS 4D-VASTLY B-GEORGE CARLIN

74 1A-SIENNA 5A-SPLIT 6A-PLAIN 7A-NEWEST 1D-SESAME 2D-ECLIPSE 3D-NITRATE 4D-PEANUT B-PAUL NEWMAN

75 1A-REVOKE 5A-MELON 6A-AGENT 7A-METHOD 1D-REMARK 2D-VILLAGE 3D-KENNETH 4D-ROUTED B-ROADRUNNER

76 1A-PUPPET 5A-MISER 6A-UTTER 7A-BEACON 1D-PUMPED 2D-POSTURE 3D-ERRATIC 4D-WARREN B-RODENTS

77 1A-ENTICE 5A-BORON 6A-ALERT 7A-HOSTEL 1D-EMBARK 2D-TORNADO 3D-CONNECT 4D-RENTAL B-RHINOCEROS

78 1A-ORPHAN 5A-TURNS 6A-INNER 7A-STACKS 1D-OPTICS 2D-PERSIST 3D-ARSENIC 4D-FERRIS B-UNION PACIFIC

79 1A-BALSAM 5A-LOWER 6A-UNION 7A-OTTERS 1D-BALLOT 2D-LAWSUIT 3D-AIRLINE 4D-BLENDS B-WIMBLEDON

80 1A-PANAMA 5A-VIGOR 6A-ENACT 7A-STODGY 1D-PAVLOV 2D-NEGLECT 3D-MERMAID 4D-SENTRY B-SAO PAOLO

81 1A-GAINED 5A-RAMBO 6A-NOISE 7A-HEDGES 1D-GARTER 2D-IMMENSE 3D-EVOKING 4D-DOZENS B-HONG KONG

82 1A-MANTIS 5A-YACHT 6A-EXUDE 7A-GREETS 1D-MAYORS 2D-NUCLEAR 3D-INTRUDE 4D-PLIERS B-PORTUGAL

83 1A-CONDOR 5A-SLUNG 6A-RINSE 7A-SLACKS 1D-CASHEW 2D-NEUTRAL 3D-ORGANIC 4D-ATHENS B-LISTERINE

84 1A-IGUANA 5A-CHASM 6A-INDIA 7A-REACTS 1D-ITCHED 2D-UNALIKE 3D-NOMADIC 4D-WREAKS B-TAIWAN

85 1A-RECESS 5A-ABOVE 6A-DITTO 7A-TRACKS 1D-ROASTS 2D-CHOWDER 3D-SKEPTIC 4D-TUTORS B-TABASCO

86 1A-FUTURE 5A-CLANG 6A-SWISH 7A-ATTEND 1D-FACING 2D-TRANSIT 3D-RAGTIME 4D-ORCHID B-FINLAND

87 1A-SNEEZE 5A-OMAHA 6A-ITALY 7A-VENDOR 1D-STONES 2D-EVASIVE 3D-ZEALAND 4D-LAWYER B-EISENHOWER

88 1A-JEERED 5A-LYING 6A-ERODE 7A-STASIS 1D-JOLTED 2D-EVIDENT 3D-ENGROSS 4D-ATHENS B-JOHN TRAVOLTA

89 1A-BICEPS 5A-STUMP 6A-POLKA 7A-REGRET 1D-BASALT 2D-CRUMPLE 3D-POPULAR 4D-THWART B-TAPEWORMS

90 1A-PALTRY 5A-TEMPT 6A-OZARK 7A-KNOTTY 1D-PUTRID 2D-LAMPOON 3D-RETRACT 4D-MONKEY B-NINCOMPOOP

91 1A-JACKAL 5A-RURAL 6A-MINDS 7A-OCEANS 1D-JERSEY 2D-CERAMIC 3D-ATLANTA 4D-TRUSTS B-SRI LANKA

92 1A-DELUGE 5A-MOCHA 6A-NUDGE 7A-FEMALE 1D-DOMAIN 2D-LICENSE 3D-GRANDPA 4D-SLEEVE B-FILLMORE

93 1A-CRANKY 5A-ROCKY 6A-UNTIE 7A-STANZA 1D-CORTEX 2D-ACCOUNT 3D-KRYPTON 4D-CINEMA B-KARAOKE

94 1A-MOSAIC 5A-GLOAT 6A-PARIS 7A-FORMED 1D-MAGNUM 2D-SCORPIO 3D-INTERIM 4D-ABUSED B-POLAR BEAR

95 1A-INCOME 5A-JOUST 6A-PARTY 7A-VENDOR 1D-INJECT 2D-CRUMPLE 3D-MATURED 4D-LAWYER B-JIMMY CARTER

96 1A-COFFIN 5A-HOARD 6A-CRAFT 7A-REWARD 1D-COHERE 2D-FIANCEE 3D-INDIANA 4D-JOLTED B-RON HOWARD

97 1A-BLOTCH 5A-TAFFY 6A-ENTER 7A-STUCCO 1D-BOTHER 2D-OFFBEAT 3D-CRYPTIC 4D-HAIRDO B-TORONTO

98 1A-SUBDUE 5A-FLOCK 6A-TEMPO 7A-GRATIS 1D-SAFARI 2D-BOOSTER 3D-UNKEMPT 4D-SHOOTS B-GARTH BROOKS

99 1A-BUNION 5A-KITES 6A-LYRIC 7A-DEFEAT 1D-BAKERY 2D-NATALIE 3D-OBSERVE 4D-BOBCAT B-BOB BARKER

100 1A-REMOVE 5A-TENSE 6A-TONIC 7A-CRIMES 1D-RATION 2D-MONITOR 3D-VIETNAM 4D-SLACKS B-OREO COOKIES

COLLECT THESE FUN PUZZLES IN THE POCKET POSH® SERIES!

Sudoku
Killer Sudoku
Easy Sudoku
Large Print Sudoku
London Sudoku
New York Sudoku
San Francisco Sudoku
Christmas Sudoku
Christmas Easy Sudoku
Girl Sudoku
Hanukkah Sudoku
Thomas Kinkade Sudoku
Thomas Kinkade Sudoku with Scripture
Shopaholic's Sudoku
Sudoku & Beyond
Code Number Sudoku
Sudoku Fusion
Wonderword™
Word Roundup™
Word Roundup™ Hollywood
Large Print Word Roundup™
Christmas Word Roundup™
Word Roundup™ Challenge
Christmas Word Roundup™ Challenge
Crosswords
Christmas Crosswords
Girl Crosswords
Hanukkah Crosswords
Thomas Kinkade Crosswords
Thomas Kinkade Crosswords with Scripture
New York Crosswords
Jumble® Crosswords
Jumble® BrainBusters
Double Jumble®
Bible Jumble®
Word Search
Girl Word Search
WORDScrimmage™
Left Brain/Right Brain
Logic
Christmas Logic
Hangman
Girl Hangman
Hidato®
Mazematics
Sukendo®
Brain Games
Christmas Brain Games
Codewords
One-Minute Puzzles
Jane Austen Puzzles & Quizzes
William Shakespeare Puzzles & Quizzes
Charles Dickens Puzzles & Quizzes
Irish Puzzles & Quizzes
London Puzzles & Quizzes
J. R. R. Tolkien Puzzles & Quizzes
Sherlock Holmes Puzzles & Quizzes
King James Puzzles
Petite Pocket Posh® Sudoku
Petite Pocket Posh® Crosswords
Petite Pocket Posh® Word Roundup™
Word Puzzles
Mom's Games to Play with Your Kids (Ages 4–6 & 7–12)
Cryptograms
Almost Impossible Number Puzzles
Almost Impossible Word Puzzles
Word Lover's Puzzle & Quiz Book
Lateral Thinking
The New York Times Brain Games
Quick Thinking
Logical Thinking
Memory Games
Cat Lover's Puzzle & Quiz Book